Batsford Chess Library

Tactics in the Sicilian

GENNADY NESIS with
Professor Igor Blekhtsin

Translated by Malcolm Gesthuysen

An Owl Book
Henry Holt and Company
New York

Henry Holt and Company, Inc.
Publishers since 1866
115 West 18th Street
New York, New York 10011

Henry Holt® is a registered trademark
of Henry Holt and Company, Inc.

First published in the United States in 1993 by
Henry Holt and Company, Inc.
Originally published in Great Britain in 1993 by
B. T. Batsford Ltd.

Library of Congress Catalog Card Number: 93-77850

ISBN 0-8050-2934-6 (An Owl Book: pbk.)

First American Edition—1993

Printed in the United Kingdom
All first editions are printed on acid-free paper. ∞

10 9 8 7 6 5 4 3 2 1

Adviser: R. D. Keene, GM, OBE
Technical Editor: Andrew Kinsman

Contents

Introduction

Many years of practical experience playing the same systems of the Sicilian Defence (especially the Dragon Variation) in major correspondence competition have led me to conclude that for the study of modern openings it is very useful to single out the tactical ideas and methods which most characterise each particular system.

The classification of tactical ideas can play a very important role in getting to know an opening, and this is particularly true of an opening as double-edged and dynamic as the Sicilian Defence. Such an approach to the study of openings greatly enhances one's intuitive perception of the opening phase of the game, and it also introduces an easily-grasped theoretical aspect to take the place of routine memorising of complex variations.

The first two books in this series were devoted to closed games. Tactical motifs play an important role in closed games such as the King's Indian Defence and the Grünfeld Defence, and the approach suggested for studying these openings seemed to us entirely justified. So it was a logical continuation to turn to an opening as complex and varied as the Sicilian Defence.

The Sicilian Defence, which basically comprises several independent opening systems, has been the most popular chess opening for many years. A particular feature of this opening is that it requires exceptionally accurate and active play from both sides right from the start. The tactical nature of most of the popular Sicilian systems is determined by the necessity to get a lead in development in an asymmetrical position, and the role played by tactics is particularly important in positions where castling has taken place on opposite sides of the board, a frequent occurrence in many variations of this defence.

During the last few decades ideas from Sicilian middlegames, characteristic of positions where both sides are fully developed, have increasingly found their way into the opening phase of the game. As Grandmaster Suetin has observed, the fight for the initiative in the opening is full of sharp, tactical combinations. This is particularly true of a number of Sicilian variations in which tactical play is becoming more and more significant. The modern approach, involving very sharp play, has encouraged an increase in the popularity of systems where castling takes place on opposite sides, systems in which the bold plans of one player are taken on uncompromisingly by his opponent.

In many Sicilian systems an attack on a castled position is quite often accompanied right from the start by the sacrifice of pawns — or even a piece — with the aim of opening lines as quickly as possible. For example, in the main variation of the Rauzer System (1 e4 c5 2 ♘f3 ♘c6 3 d4 cd 4 ♘xd4 ♘f6 5 ♘c3 d6 6 ♗g5 e6 7 ♕d2 ♗e7 8 0–0–0 0–0) after 9 f4 ♘xd4 10 ♕xd4 ♕a5 11 ♕d2 h6 a common continuation is 12 h4, sacrificing a piece for the sake of opening the h-file.

Also very characteristic in this regard is the popular standard position arising in the Dragon Variation (1 e4 c5 2 ♘f3 d6 3 d4 cd 4 ♘xd4 ♘f6 5 ♘c3 g6 6 ♗e3 ♗g7 7 f3 ♘c6 8 ♕d2 0–0 9 ♗c4 ♗d7 10 0–0–0 ♖c8 11 ♗b3 ♘e5 12 h4 ♘c4 13 ♗xc4 ♖xc4). Here too, White as a rule sacrifices a pawn with the same aim as in the previous example — to open the h-file: 14 h5 ♘xh5 15 g4 ♘f6. In this well-known position White has tried numerous plans. For example, there is an interesting sacrifice of another pawn, but this time with the aim of opening the central d-file: 16 e5 de 17 ♘b3 ♖c6. In order to demonstrate the role of tactics in this system I shall quote a few more moves from the game Wibe–Nesis (corr. Ol. 1989/91): 18 ♗c5 h6!? 19 ♖xh6!? b6 20 ♖h4 bc 21 ♕h2 ♖e8 22 ♖h1 ♔f8 23 ♖h8+ ♘g8 24 ♖h7 g5! 25 ♘xc5 ♗c8 26 ♖xg7 ♔xg7 27 ♕xe5+ ♔f8 28 ♖h7 ♖g6 29 ♘e4 f6, and Black beat off the attack, retaining a big lead in material.

Although play after castling on opposite sides usually involves attacks on the flanks, it is also essential to keep in mind the possibility of transferring play to the centre. The sharpest tactical battles develop in those cases where the pawn structure in the centre is still unclear. We shall again refer to the Yugoslav Attack in the Dragon Variation (1 e4 c5 2 ♘f3 d6 3 d4 cd 4 ♘xd4 ♘f6 5 ♘c3 g6 6 ♗e3 ♗g7 7 f3 0–0 8 ♕d2 ♘c6). For a long time the main continuation in this position was 9 0–0–0 ♘xd4. But then a sharp counter-punch in the centre became fashionable: 9 ...

d5!?. Here it is Black who sacrifices a pawn for the sake of opening up lines as quickly as possible on the queenside, where the white king has taken refuge.

Other, similar examples might be quoted, but it is already clear how important tactics can be in an opening as dynamic and double-edged as the Sicilian Defence.

Before we move on to the main body of text, we should say a few words about the way in which the book has been structured. The first four chapters deal primarily with direct attacks on one or other of the kings, according to whether and on what side castling has taken place. Chapters five and six deal with tactics which emerge from dynamically equal positions in which the players exchange punch and counter-punch. The final chapters of the book deal with familiar specific tactics which occur time and again in Sicilian positions: enticement, deflection, interference, the pin, the back rank, the intermediate move and combinations of these tactics.

I believe that familiarity with typical tactical methods in the Sicilian will help chess-lovers not only to understand and study the theory and practice of the Sicilian Defence more profoundly, but also to improve their all-round tactical ability.

G. Nesis
June 1992

1 Attacking after Kingside Castling by Both Players

The attacking side in these cases seeks to maximize the pressure on the opposing king. Where possible, the aim is to build up a mating attack or to achieve substantial gain of material.

The following considerations are essential: firstly, to overcome the resistance of the opposing pieces, by forcing them to retreat in the face of a pawn onslaught, or to be exchanged; secondly, to wreck or compromise the enemy king's pawn cover; thirdly, one should not allow the position of one's own king to be substantially weakened.

There are various positional and tactical methods for solving these tasks; in particular, the castled position of the enemy king can be weakened with the aid of a pawn offensive, which at the same time can bring about the opening of lines along which the attacking side's pieces can tear into the heart of the enemy king's position.

A typical example of this plan occurred in the game Geller–Anikaev, Minsk 1979, in which the Scheveningen Variation was played (*see diagram overleaf*).

Geller–Anikaev
Minsk 1979

Thanks to his control of the central squares, and not fearing the counter-thrust d6–d5, White proceeds to launch a pawn storm.

13 g4!   ♖fc8

In the event of 13 ... ♘c4 White could have played a very promising piece sacrifice: 14 g5 ♘e8 15 ♘f5! ♗d8 16 ♗d4! ef 17 ♘d5 ♕c8 18 ♖ae1 fe 19 ♗xe4 with a very strong attack.

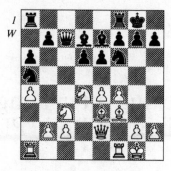

14 g5

A serious defect of Black's position is the absence from the centre of his queen's knight, which should occupy the key square e5.

14 ... ♘e8

15 f5

White's pawn storm gathers momentum.

15 ... ♘c4

16 ♗h5!

This is the first real threat (17 ♗xf7+), forcing Black to weaken his position. It should be noted that the black pieces are rather inactive and, in addition, get in each other's way. On the other hand, the white pieces are bearing down on the enemy king.

16 ... g6

17 fg fg

18 ♕f2 ♘e5

19 ♘f3!

White exchanges off the main piece defending the black king, after which Black's position becomes indefensible.

19 ... ♘g7

Black would also lose after 21 ... gh 22 ♘xe5 de 23 ♕f7+ ♔h8 24 ♕xe7 ♘g7 25 ♖f7.

20 ♘xe5 ♖f8

21 ♘f7 ♘xh5 *(2)*

The game has approached a climax. A brilliant combination now follows.

22 ♘d5!!

Clearing the a1–h8 diagonal once and for all: Black will no

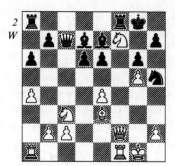

longer have the move ... e6–e5.

22	...	ed
23	♘h6+	♔g7
24	♕f7+!	♖xf7
25	♖xf7+	♔h8
26	♗d4+	♗f6
27	♖xf6!	Black resigned.

On 27 ... ♘g7 there would follow 28 ♖f7 ♖g8 29 ♗xg7+ ♖xg7 30 ♖f8+ with mate.

This brilliant game is a classic example of a Sicilian attack after both players have castled on the same side.

The other examples included in this chapter are also rather typical. In these games many tactical methods and tricks are employed, both during the course of a storm (in several cases a whole cascade of sacrifices is encountered, with the aim of destroying the king's protective screen and opening lines) and at the conclusive stage.

Game No. 1
Gufeld–Osnos
Tbilisi 1978

1	e4	c5
2	♘f3	♘f6

This move leads to a defensive system worked out by Rubinstein. It was Nimzowitsch who first started playing it, but after 3 e5 he retreated the knight to g8, after which Black has lost two tempi.

3 e5

After 3 ♘c3 one possibility is 3 ... d6. Continuations leading to an interesting struggle with chances for both sides are: 3 ... d5 4 ed ♘xd5 5 ♗b5+ ♘c6! (but not 5 ... ♗d7? because of 6 ♘e5! ♗xb5 7 ♕f3!) 6 ♘e5 ♘xc3 7 dc!, or 3 ... ♘c6 4 d4 d5 5 ed ♘xd5.

| | 3 | ... | ♘d5 |
| | 4 | d4 | |

In principle the most testing move is 4 ♘c3, as in Game 7; Michell–Nimzowitsch, which leads to very sharp and complicated play. The move 4 c4 does not pose substantial difficulties for Black: after 4 ... ♘c7 5 d4 cd 6 ♕xd4 ♘c6 7 ♕e4 d5 8 ed ♕xd6 9 ♘c3 ♕g6! he has an excellent position.

4	...	cd
5	♕xd4	e6
6	♗c4	♘c6

More precise is 6 ... d6!, in order after 7 ♗xd5 to reply 7 ... de 8 ♕xe5 ♕xd5, with approximate equality.

| 7 | ♕e4 | d6 |
| 8 | 0–0 | |

On 8 ed Black plays the intermediate 8 ... ♘f6.

| 8 | ... | de |
| 9 | ♘xe5 | ♕c7 |

The immediate transition to an ending with 9 ... ♘f6 10 ♘xc6 ♘xe4 11 ♘xd8 ♔xd8 12 ♖d1+ ♔c7 leads after 13 ♗d3 ♘d6 14 c4! to a position offering Black few prospects (Martinovic–Bjelajac, Novi Sad 1978).

| 10 | ♘f3 | ♘f6 |
| 11 | ♕e2 | |

White seems to have played the opening rather modestly, but Black's game is far from easy: he remains behind in development and cramped for space, and he is losing the battle for the centre.

11	...	♗d6
12	♖e1	♘g4
13	h3	♘ge5
14	♘xe5	♗xe5

Worth considering was 14 ... ♘xe5 15 ♗b5+ ♗d7.

| 15 | ♘d2 | 0–0 |
| 16 | ♘f3 | ♘d4 |

Black has been tempted by a tactical possibility to exchange knights (it is bad for White to play 17 ♕xe5 because of 17 ... ♘xf3+ and 18 ... ♕xc4), but more natural was the simple retreat of the bishop to f6, with quite a solid position.

| 17 | ♘xd4 | ♗xd4 |

	18	♖d1	♗c5

The bishop is heading for f8, but this plan is too passive: it looks more forceful for Black to play 18 ... e5.

	19	b3!	

Immediately occupying the vacated diagonal.

	19	...	♗d7
	20	♗b2	♖fd8
	21	♕g4	♗f8
	22	♗f6!	

An unpleasant move for Black, setting him a specific problem: to where should he retreat his rook on d8?

	22	...	♖e8?!

A tactical error; if Black could have seen into the future he would have moved the rook to c8. But at this moment it was difficult to foresee that it was essential to defend the black queen.

	23	♗d3	♗c6 *(3)*

Also after the relatively best 23 ... ♖ac8 24 h4! Black would have been doomed to defend a difficult position.

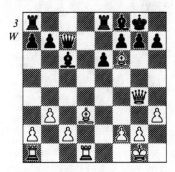

	24	♗xh7+!	

A very familiar sacrifice, but operations to destroy the king's pawn cover are rarely encountered in this kind of position.

	24	...	♔xh7
	25	♕h5+	♔g8 *(4)*
	26	♖d4!	

This move is the point of the combination. White leaves his other bishop *en prise* and brings his rook into the attack, creating the threat of mate: ♖d4–h4.

	26	...	gf
	27	♖g4+	♗g7

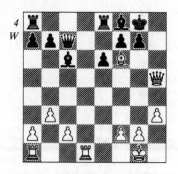

28	**♕h6**	**♚f8**
29	**♖xg7!** *(5)*	

This is the way to do it! Now White threatens to capture the pawn on f7 (with double check!), followed by check with the queen on h7, after which the undefended position of the black queen will be the decisive factor.

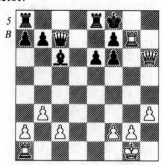

29	**...**	**♖ac8**

Other continuations would not have saved the game (as can be seen from analysis by Gufeld): 29 ... ♕d8 30 ♕h7! ♕d7 31 ♕g8+; 29 ... ♖ec8 30 ♕xf6 ♗e4 31 ♖e1! ♗xc2 32 ♕g5! (threatening 33 ♖g8 mate) 32 ... ♗g6 33 ♕h6; 29 ... ♗e4 30 ♖g4+ ♚e7 31 ♖xe4 ♕xc2 32 ♖c4 and 33 ♖ac1; and 29 ... ♕d7 30 ♕xf6 ♗e4 31 ♕g5!.

30	**♕h7!**

Now the threat of ♕g8+ is extremely unpleasant, particularly since it is reinforced by the possibility of a preliminary 31 ♖d1!, cutting off the black king.

30	**...**	**b5**

Now in the event of the hasty 31 ♕g8+ ♚e7 there does not

appear to be a way for White to end the game. He can give a lot of checks, but in each case Black escapes from immediate danger at the cost of not particularly significant loss of material.

31	♖d1!	♗d5
32	c4!	bc
33	bc	

It is not possible for Black to capture this impudent pawn, because of mate. The bishop is doomed, and further resistance would be futile, so Black resigned.

Game No. 2
Stein–Portisch
Stockholm 1962

1	e4	c5
2	♘f3	e6
3	d4	cd
4	♘xd4	a6
5	♗d3	♘f6
6	0–0	♕c7

As is also the case with 6 ... d6, Black prevents the move e4–e5. Sometimes this continuation amounts to mere transposition after a subsequent ... d7–d6.

7	♘d2

This way of developing the knight is no better than the usual move, ♘c3. The most logical continuation, with the aid of which White renews the threat of e4–e5, is 7 ♕e2 (see Game 60; Mainka–Lau).

7	...	♘c6

The game Velimirovic–Ljubojevic, Yugoslavia 1980, continued: 7 ... ♗e7 8 a4 ♘c6 9 ♘xc6 bc 10 b3 d5 11 ♗b2 0–0 12 e5 ♘d7 13 ♕h5 g6 14 ♕h6 c5 (better is 14 ... ♖e8 immediately, leaving the c5-square for the knight) 15 ♖ae1 ♖e8 16 ♘f3 ♗f8 17 ♕h4 ♗g7, with complicated play.

8	♘xc6	bc

Other possibilities are less acceptable: 8 ... ♕xc6 9 e5!, or 8 ... dc 9 f4 ♗c5+ 10 ♔h1 0–0 11 e5 ♘d5 12 ♘e4; in both cases the pawn on e5 cramps Black very considerably.

9	f4	♗c5+?

This natural check is the main cause of all Black's difficulties. Stein called this move 'an illusory gain of a tempo', rightly considering that the dark-squared bishop should be placed on e7 in order to fulfil defensive duties. Better was 9 ... d5, although also in this case White retains some initiative by playing 10 ♕e2 ♗e7 11 b3 0–0 12 ♗b2.

	10	♔h1	d6

Now it would be bad to play 10 ... d5, in view of 11 e5 ♘d7 12 ♕g4!.

	11	♘f3	e5

It would not have been good to play 11 ... 0–0, because of 12 e5! de 13 fe ♘d5 14 ♗xh7+ with a decisive attack.

	12	fe	de
	13	♘h4	0–0
	14	♘f5	♗e6

The lesser evil was the immediate elimination of the troublesome white knight. But also after 14 ... ♗xf5 15 ♖xf5 ♘e8 16 ♕g4 ♕e7 17 ♕g3 White retains a serious initiative.

	15	♕e2	a5
	16	♗c4!	

Preventing the consolidating move ... f7–f6 after the black knight moves away from f6.

	16	...	♔h8
	17	♗g5	♘d7?

In Stein's opinion this was the decisive mistake, since the knight is moved away from the defence of the black king. He considered that it was only possible for Black to put up a defence — albeit a passive one — by playing 17 ... ♘g8.

	18	♖ad1	♘b6 (6)

Also after 18 ... ♗xc4 19 ♕xc4 f6 20 ♗h4 Black's position is not one to be happy with.

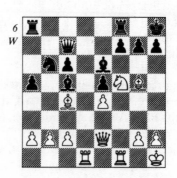

19	♘xg7!!	♗xc4

Taking the knight also leads to a quick mate: 19 ... ♔xg7 20 ♗f6+ ♔g8 21 ♕f3 ♕c8 22 ♕g3+ ♗g4 23 ♖f5.

20	♗f6!!	♗e7

The threat was 21 ♘f5+ ♔g8 22 ♘h6 mate.

21	♕f3 *(7)*

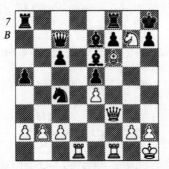

On 21 ... ♔g8 there could follow 22 ♘h5 ♖fc8 23 ♕g3+ ♔f8 24 ♕g7+ ♔e8 25 ♕g8+ ♗f8 26 ♘g7 mate.

Black resigned.

A little masterpiece.

Game No. 3
Kovallik–Blekhtsin
Dortmund 1991

1	e4	c5
2	♘f3	e6
3	d4	cd
4	♘xd4	♕b6!?

This move is rarely seen, but White has to play accurately.

5	♘b3	♗b4+
6	c3	

Worth considering is 6 ♗d2, with the possible continuation 6 ... ♗xd2+ 7 ♘1xd2 d5 8 ♕g4, when White has a definite advantage.

6	...	♗e7
7	♗e3	♕c7
8	f4	♘f6
9	♗d3	b6
10	0–0	♗b7

	11	♘1d2	d6

Black has coped with his opening task successfully and has obtained quite a comfortable Scheveningen-type position.

	12	♔h1	♘bd7
	13	♕e2	0–0
	14	♗g1	e5

A natural reaction to the passive retreat of the white bishop.

	15	h3	ef

Black mistakenly relaxes his control over the important d4-square. Quieter was 15 ... d5 16 fe ♘xe4 17 ♘xe4 de 18 ♗xe4 ♕xe5, with an equal game.

	16	♖xf4	d5
	17	♖f5	♗d6
	18	♗d4	♖fe8
	19	♖af1	de
	20	♗b5	e3

Black has underestimated White's tactical possibilities. Worth considering was 20 ... ♗c6, although also in this case after 21 ♗xc6 ♕xc6 22 ♘c4 White's initiative entirely offsets the sacrificed pawn.

	21	♘c4	♘e4 *(8)*

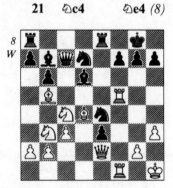

	22	♕xe3!!	

A superb, stunning queen sacrifice!

	22	...	♘g3+
	23	♕xg3	♗xg3
	24	♖xf7 *(9)*	

A rather curious position: White has just one minor piece for his queen, but nevertheless it is not easy for Black to find a defence against White's threats.

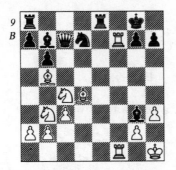

24	...	♗xg2+!
25	♔xg2	♖e2+
26	♔g1!	

In the event of 26 ♔h1 Black would seize the initiative with 26 ... ♖h2+ 27 ♔g1 ♗f2+!! 28 ♖1xf2 (on 28 ♗xf2 Black wins with 28 ... ♖xh3) 28 ... ♕g3+ 29 ♔f1 ♕xh3+ 30 ♔e1 ♘e5!.

| 26 | ... | ♗e5 |

The only move.

27	♘xe5	♖xe5
28	♗xe5	♕xe5
29	♗xd7	h5

Despite White's big advantage in material, the open position of his king gives Black definite chances to save the game.

30	♘d4	♖d8
31	♗c6	♖d6
32	♖f8+	♔h7
33	♗g2	♖g6
34	♖8f3	♕d5
35	b3	

More accurate was 35 a3.

35	...	b5
36	♖1f2	♕e4
37	♖f5	♕e1+
38	♔h2	♔h6

The black pieces have taken up such active positions that White's chances of turning his extra material into victory are very slim. Besides, he now overlooks a double attack.

| 39 | ♘xb5 | ♖g5 |
| 40 | ♖xg5? | ♔xg5 |

41	♖f3

Another mistake. White could have guaranteed a draw by playing 41 ♖f7 ♛e5+ 42 ♔h1 ♛xb5 43 ♖xg7+.

41	...	♛e5+
42	♔g1	♛xb5
43	c4	♛e5

Black won after a few more moves.

Game No. 4
J. Polgar–Hulak
Amsterdam 1989

1	e4	c5
2	♘f3	e6
3	d4	cd
4	♘xd4	♘c6
5	♘c3	♛c7
6	♗e2	a6
7	0-0	♘f6
8	♗e3	♗e7
9	f4	d6

Both players had the opportunity to choose a wide variety of systems, but in the end they have arrived at one of the typical positions arising from the Scheveningen Variation.

10	♛e1	♗d7

10 ... 0–0 11 ♖d1 ♗d7 12 ♛g3 is considered in the next game, Geller-Yap.

11	♛g3	0-0
12	♖ae1	b5
13	a3	♘xd4
14	♗xd4	♗c6
15	♗d3	♖ab8

This move does not look good, but also after 15 ... e5 16 fe ♘h5 17 ♛f3 de 18 ♘d5! White has the better position.

16	e5	♘e8
17	f5	

The white pieces look very menacing, but such positions occur very often in tournament play nowadays, and White's attack by no means always proves successful.

17	...	ef
18	♖xf5	de *(10)*

Played in the hope that after the natural 19 ♗xe5 ♗d6 a sequence of exchanges will begin and the black king will turn out to be completely safe, but the 13-year-old girl's reply came as a complete surprise to the experienced Grandmaster.

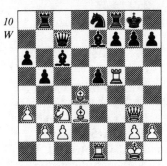

19   ♕h3!!

Now if 19 ... ed then 20 ♖xf7!, and after either capture Black is mated: 20 ... ♔xf7 21 ♕e6 mate, or 20 ... ♖xf7 21 ♕xh7+ ♔f8 22 ♕h8 mate. No use either is 20 ... h6 because of 21 ♖exe7 ♕d6 22 ♕f5. In the event of 19 ... g6 a spectacular finale is possible: 20 ♗xe5 ♗d6 21 ♕xh7+! ♔xh7 22 ♖h5+ ♔g8 23 ♖h8 mate.

19   ...   h6

The only playable continuation.

20   ♗xe5   ♕a7+
21   ♔h1   ♗d6 *(11)*

22   ♖g5!

Yet more tactics! On 22 ... ♗xe5 decisive is 23 ♕xh6 g6 24 ♖h5!. Now White threatens not only to capture the pawn on h6 with the queen, but also 23 ♗xg7.

| 22 | ... | ♛f2! |

The only way to try to alter the character of the game.

23	♖f1	♛xf1+
24	♗xf1	hg
25	♗d3	

The second phase of the attack begins.

25	...	f5
26	♗xf5!	♗xe5
27	♛h7+	♔f7
28	♛g6+	♔e7

Of course, not 28 ... ♔g8 because of 29 ♗e6+.

| 29 | ♛e6+ | ♔d8 |
| 30 | ♛xe5 | |

White's lead in material is not great, but Black's problem is that his pieces are so badly coordinated.

30	...	♖b7
31	♔g1	♖bf7
32	g4	g6
33	♛b8+	♔e7 *(12)*

The impression is that Black has been quite successful, but now comes another very nice tactical trick.

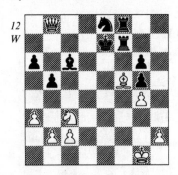

| 34 | ♘d5+! | |

The black bishop is enticed onto the d5-square, where it will be taken with check.

34	...	♗xd5
35	♛e5+	♔d8
36	♛xd5+	♔c7

Black's position would also be bad after 36 ... ♔e7 37 ♛d7+ ♔f6 38 ♛e6+ ♔g7 39 ♛xg6+ ♔h8 40 ♛h6+ ♔g8 41 ♗e6.

	37	♕c5+	♔b8

Or 37 ... ♔d8 38 ♕c8+ ♔e7 39 ♕d7+.

	38	♕b6+	♖b7
	39	♕d8+	♔a7
	40	♗xg6	

The black knight is defenceless.
Black resigned.

Game No. 5
Geller–Yap
Moscow 1986

1	e4	c5
2	♘f3	e6
3	d4	cd
4	♘xd4	♘c6
5	♘c3	a6
6	♗e2	♕c7
7	0–0	♘f6
8	♗e3	♗e7
9	f4	d6
10	♕e1	0–0
11	♖d1	♗d7
12	♕g3	♖ac8
13	♔h1	b5
14	e5	

A typical pawn sacrifice in such positions: now in the event of
14 ... de 15 fe ♘xe5 (15 ... ♕xe5 loses immediately, because of 16
♘xc6) 16 ♗f4 ♗d6 17 ♘dxb5! ab 18 ♖xd6! White gets a big
advantage.

14	...	♘e8
15	♘e4	d5?

A serious positional error. Black releases the tension in the
centre and so makes it quite safe for White to attack. Geller
considers that Black should have played 15 ... de 16 fe f5, with a
complicated game.

16	♘g5	♘xd4
17	♗xd4	h6 *(13)*

Black was counting on being able to capture the pawn on c2
with his queen after the white knight retreats; after this White's
compensation would not look too significant, but there now

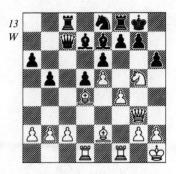

13
W

followed a veritable cascade of sacrifices, totally wrecking the black king's position.

18 &d3! g6 (14)

Alas, the knight cannot be captured. On 18 ... hg White had planned to play 19 fg g6 (otherwise 20 g6) 20 ♕h4 ♕d8 21 ♖f6! ♘g7 22 ♕h6, and Black is defenceless against the manoeuvre ♖d1–f1–f3–h3.

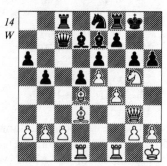

14
W

19 ♘xe6! &xe6

Capturing the knight with the pawn leads to mate in three: 20 ♕xg6+ ♘g7 21 ♕h7+ ♔f7 22 &g6 mate.

20 f5 ♘g7

Geller considers that an attempt by Black to hold on to the piece would not have brought any let-up in the attack: 20 ... &d7 21 fg f5 22 h4, or even 22 &e3 ♔g7 23 ♕h3 ♖h8 24 &xf5!.

21 fe ♘xe6 (15)

And now comes another tactical trick, but this time a decisive one: Black's position falls apart.

22 ♖xf7! ♖xf7
23 ♕xg6+ ♔f8

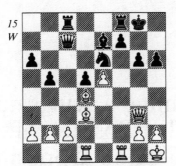

| | 24 | ♕xh6+! | ♚e8 |

Black cannot save the knight (24 ... ♘g7) because of 25 ♕h8 mate.

| | 25 | ♕xe6 | ♕c6 |
| | 26 | ♕g6 | |

With the threat of 27 e6.

	26	...	♕xg6
	27	♗xg6	♚f8
	28	♗xf7	♚xf7
	29	c3	Black resigned.

2 Storming a Kingside Castled Position after Castling on Opposite Sides

Pawn storms after castling has taken place on opposite sides of the board are usually double-edged, and a great deal depends on the time-factor.

Tactics during such storms are employed most frequently, particularly at the conclusive stage of an attack, after the king's position has been wrecked and a king-hunt is on. But situations are quite often encountered in which it is impossible to accomplish a strategic plan without the aid of tactics. In these cases the attacking side can bring about the right conditions for storming the king with the aid of intuitive sacrifices.

A pawn storm in conjunction with castling long is a very common plan for White in most Sicilian systems. White removes his king to the queenside, and his pieces are posted so that they can control the centre and can also be transferred at any time to the kingside. If these conditions are satisfied, a pawn storm directed at the black king's position can be extremely effective. The white pawns loosen the defensive fortifications, and the white pieces act as battering-rams.

Practice has shown that passive defence (and this is the case in the majority of the games in this chapter) can have sad consequences. If the defending side does not manage to develop a counter-offensive the attack can be crushing in a very short time. For example, the game Lukin–Shirov (see below) never even reached the conclusive phase of the storm.

It should be noted, however, that it is not always necessary to launch a pawn storm after castling on opposite sides — sometimes it is more effective to carry out a piece attack.

It is a characteristic of Sicilian games that storms of kingside castled positions are carried out not only by White but also by Black. In Games 6, 7 and 9 Black took — at first sight — a risky decision by castling long, but it only required slight delay by White for Black to be able to aim his pieces at the white king and to create a series of dangerous threats. This resulted in all the necessary conditions for carrying out tactical operations, finally resulting in disaster for White.

Lukin–Shirov
Daugavpils 1989

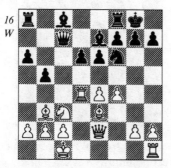

This game began with one of the sharpest variations of the Sozin Attack. White now offers a pawn, not losing a tempo in playing 13 ♖f1.

13	f5!	ef
14	ef	♗xf5
15	g4	♗e6
16	g5	♘d7
17	♕h5	♗f5?

Worth considering was 17 ... ♖fc8 18 ♖h4 ♘f8.

18	♖f1	♗g6
19	♕d1	

Now the h-pawn is ready for a decisive storm.

19	...	♘c5
20	♗d5	♖ab8
21	h4	b4
22	h5	

Not reducing the pace of the attack.

| 22 | ... | ♗xc2 |

More chances of saving the game were offered by playing 22

... bc 23 hg cb+ (worse is 23 ... ♖xb2 24 ♗xf7+ ♔h8 25 ♕h5)
24 ♔b1 hg, although here too White has a very strong attack
after 25 ♕f3 or 25 ♕g4.

23	♕xc2	bc
24	♕xc3	♘e6
25	♖c4	♕d7
26	h6	♗d8
27	g6!!	*(17)*

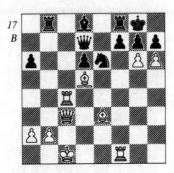

After this bayonet thrust from White a very picturesque position
has arisen. The threat is simply 28 ♗xe6. On 27 ... hg there follows
28 ♗xe6 fe 29 ♖xf8+ ♔xf8 30 h7; also bad is 27 ... gh 28 ♗xh6.
Black resigned.

Game No. 6
Ljubojevic–Kasparov
Linares 1991

1	e4	c5
2	♘c3	d6
3	f4	♘c6
4	♘f3	g6
5	♗b5	♗d7
6	0–0	♗g7
7	d3	

The system White has chosen does not give him serious grounds
for obtaining an opening advantage. Nevertheless, a certain degree
of accuracy is required from Black.

7	...	a6
8	♗xc6	♗xc6
9	♕e1	♕d7

Black does not hurry to determine the position of his king's knight, and he is 'threatening' to castle long.

10	a4	b6
11	b3	

A rather slow plan. Worth considering was 11 e5.

11	...	♘f6
12	h3	♘h5!
13	♗d2	f5
14	ef?	

It is difficult to agree with this decision, since it creates favourable possibilities for Black to launch kingside attack utilising both the g-file and the h1–a8 diagonal.

14	...	gf
15	♕h4	♘f6
16	♖ae1	0-0-0
17	a5	b5
18	b4	

White's position is not very promising, and so this attempt to complicate the game is understandable.

On 18 ♘g5, Black would have had the unpleasant reply 18 ... ♖hg8.

18	...	cb
19	♘a2	♘d5
20	♘xb4	♗f6
21	♕f2	♘xb4
22	♗xb4	♖hg8

Now Black has a simple and clear plan of action: all his pieces are going to bear down on the white king.

23	♖e2	♖g6
24	♕e1	♖dg8
25	♔h2	e5!

Another diagonal is opened up.

26	fe	♗xe5+
27	♔h1	♕b7

It is not clear why Black preferred this move to the simple 27 ... ♕g7; if 28 ♕f2 then 28 ... ♕h6 would be decisive, and if 28 ♕d2 then 28 ... ♖g3.

28 d4 *(18)*

Black cannot capture the pawn on d4 because of 29 ♖e7 ♗xf3 30 ♖e8+ ♖xe8 31 ♕xe8+ with a certain draw for White. Stronger

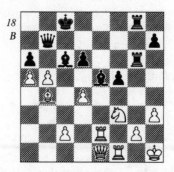

is 28 ... ♗g3 29 ♕c3 ♔b8, when Black maintains an advantage. But now the improbable happened ...

28 ... ♖xg2??

Even the greatest chessplayers make incomprehensible blunders! In seeking to implement the correct idea, Kasparov makes a tactical miscalculation.

29 ♖xg2 ♖xg2

It turns out that the natural 29 ... ♗xf3 would lose, because of 30 ♖xf3 ♕xf3 31 ♕c3+! ♕xc3 32 ♖xg8+.

30 ♔xg2 ♕g7+

31 ♔h1 ♗f4 *(19)*

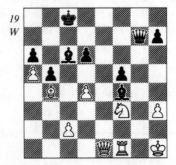

Black is a whole rook down (!), and after 32 d5 ♗xd5 33 ♕c3+ the game will immediately be over. Also not bad would be 32 ♗d2. But quite astonishing events now begin.

32 ♕e6+ ♗d7

33 ♕d5 ♕g3

Now in order to maintain winning chances White should have played 34 ♗e1 ♕xh3+ 35 ♔g1 ♗e3+ 36 ♖f2!. Also not bad was 34 ♖e1 straightaway.

34	♕a8+?	♔c7
35	♖e1	♕xh3+
36	♔g1	♕g3+
37	♔f1	♕h3+
38	♔e2	♗c6
39	♕a7+	♔c8 (20)

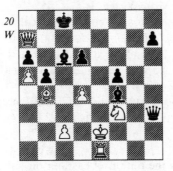

40	♖f1?

But this is a fatal error by White. He could have continued 40
d5 ♗xd5 41 ♕f2 ♗g3 42 ♖h1!.

40	...	♕g2+
41	♔e1	♗g3+!
42	♔d1	♕xf1+
43	♘e1	♗xe1

After 44 ♗xe1 there follows 44 ... ♗f3+ and White loses a
piece.

White resigned.

Game No. 7
Michell–Nimzowitsch
Marienbad 1925

1	e4	c5
2	♘f3	♘f6!?

The Nimzowitsch Variation. It was to become, as Keene has
written, the spiritual forerunner of Alekhine's Defence and is
therefore of crucial importance to an entire stream of development
in modern chess.

Nimzowitsch first adopted this variation against Spielmann in
San Sebastian (1911).

3	e5	♘d5

4	♘c3!	♘xc3

Less dangerous, according to Nimzowitsch, is 4 ... e6.

5	dc	b6

A bold move ("ultramodern", according to Nimzowitsch) — Black artificially delays his development in order to induce his opponent to reveal his cards as soon as possible — but it is extremely risky. More correct is 5 ... d5.

The move 5 ... e6 does not enjoy a particularly good reputation. For example: 6 ♗f4 ♘c6 7 ♗c4 ♕c7 8 0–0 b6 9 ♖e1! h6 10 ♘d2 d5 11 ed ♗xd6 12 ♗xd6 ♕xd6 13 ♗b5 0–0 14 ♘c4 ♕xd1 15 ♖axd1 ♘e7 16 ♘e5 with advantage to White (Keene).

6	♗d3

More energetic is 6 ♗c4 e6 7 ♗f4, and then ♕d2 and ♖d1 or 0–0–0, Also worth considering is 6 e6!? fe 7 ♘e5.

6	...	♗b7
7	♗f4	♕c7

Black reserves the option of castling on either side, as well as the creation of different types of pawn structure.

8	♗g3

Nimzowitsch preferred 8 ♕e2.

8	...	e6
9	0–0	♗e7
10	♘d2!	

An excellent centralising plan. The manoeuvre ♘d2–c4–d6+ threatens to hinder Black's development.

10	...	h5

A dubious defence, since a flank diversion is rarely strong enough to neutralise an enemy attack in the centre; therefore rather more worthy of consideration was 10 ... ♘c6 or 10 ... d5.

11	h3	g5
12	♗e4?	

Undoubtedly the strongest continuation was 12 ♘c4, and now White gets a definite advantage after either 12 ... ♘c6 13 ♘d6+ ♗xd6 14 ed ♕d8 15 ♕e2 ♕f6 16 ♗e4, or 12 ... ♘a6 13 ♕e2 0–0–0 14 ♘a5.

12	...	♘c6
13	♖e1	0–0–0
14	♘c4	

Now this manoeuvre achieves nothing.

14	...	b5!

Vacating the b6-square for the queen.

15	♘d6+	♗xd6
16	ed	♕b6
17	♗f3	*(21)*

With this move, according to Nimzowitsch, White allows the last vestige of his advantage in the centre to slip away. Correct was 17 ♗e5!, and now Black can sacrifice the exchange: 17 ... f5 18 ♗xh8 ♖xh8 19 ♗d3 g4, but after 19 ♗xc6 ♕xc6 20 f3 g4 21 ♖e5 or 21 ♖e3 he doesn't get any real compensation for the sacrificed material.

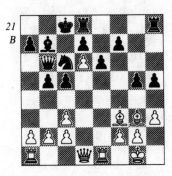

21
B

17	...	g4!

At the cost of just one pawn Black opens up two lines at once!

18	hg	hg
19	♗xg4	f5
20	♗f3	♖h7
21	♔f1	e5!

Black threatens both 22 ... e4 and 22 ... f4.

22	♗xc6	♕xc6
23	f3	e4
24	fe	♖g8
25	♗f2	fe
26	♕d2	

Intending to play 27 ♕e3, with a blockade, but it is already too late.

26	...	e3!
27	♕xe3	♕xg2+
28	♔e2	♖f7

With the threat 29 ... ♖xf2+ 30 ♕xf2 ♖e8+ 31 ♔d1, and now 31 ... ♗f3+ wins (but not 31 ... ♕xf2 immediately, because of

32 ♖xe8 mate).

	29	♔d1

The threat is mate on e8.

	29	...	♔b8
	30	♖g1 *(22)*	

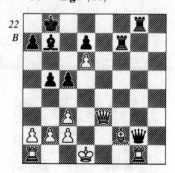

	30	...	♖xf2!

A decisive queen sacrifice.

	31	♖xg2	♖fxg2

31 ... ♖gxg2 was weaker, because of 32 ♕e8+ ♗c8 33 ♔e1.

	32	b3	♖g1+

Now Black wins easily.

	33	♔d2	♖8g2+
	34	♔d3	♖xa1
	35	♕xc5	♖d1+
	36	♔e3	♖e1+
	37	♔d3	

If 37 ♔f4 then 37 ... ♖f1+ 38 ♔e3 ♖f3+ 39 ♔d4 ♖g4+ 40 ♔e5 ♖e4 mate.

	37	...	♗e4+
	38	♔d4	♖d2+
	39	♔e5	♖d5+
	40	♕xd5	♗h1+!

White resigned.

Game No. 8
Lobron–Miles
Biel 1986

	1	e4	c5
	2	♘f3	d6

3	d4	cd
4	♘xd4	♘f6
5	♘c3	g6
6	♗c4	♗g7
7	♗e3	0-0
8	♕d2	

White has chosen a move order in which 8 ... ♘g4 is rather annoying but Black preferred to transpose to his favourite variation.

8	...	♘c6
9	f3	♗d7
10	h4	♖c8
11	♗b3	h5
12	0-0-0	♘e5
13	♗g5	♘h7

An attempt to rehabilitate the variation characterised by the move 11 ... h5, which was under a cloud at the time of this game.

14	♗h6	♗xh6
15	♕xh6	♖xc3
16	bc	♕c7 (23)

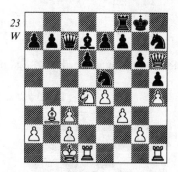

23
W

| 17 | ♔b1 | |

Now if 17 ... ♕xc3 then 18 ♘e2, winning an important tempo for the transfer of the knight to f4.

17	...	♘c4
18	g4!	hg
19	f4!	♖c8
20	♖d3	

The threat was ♘c4-a3+.

| 20 | ... | ♕a5 |
| 21 | h5 | g5 (24) |

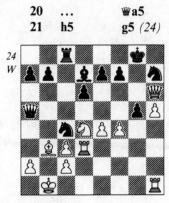

| 22 | e5! |

White carries out his attack with great vigour, not giving his opponent a moment's respite.

| 22 | ... | de |
| 23 | ♗xc4! |

But not 23 fg ed 24 g6 ♘f6, when Black's game is quite in order.

| 23 | ... | ♖xc4 |

Of course 23 ... ed would be bad, because of 24 ♗xf7+.

24	♘b3	♕c7
25	fg	♗f5
26	g6	♘f6
27	♖d2

Now it is not clear how Black can defend against an attack by the rooks down the d-file.

| 27 | ... | ♖xc3 (25) |

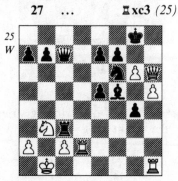

| 28 | ♖hd1! |

Simple and elegant.

28	...	♗xc2+
29	♖xc2	♖xc2
30	gf+	♔xf7
31	♕g6+	♔e6
32	♕xc2	♕xc2+
33	♔xc2	Black soon resigned.

Game No. 9
Nikitin–Tal
USSR Ch., Tbilisi 1959

1	e4	c5
2	♘f3	d6
3	d4	cd
4	♘xd4	♘f6
5	♘c3	a6
6	♗g5	♘bd7
7	♗c4	♕a5
8	♕d2	e6

The continuation 8 ... h6 9 ♗xf6 occurred in Game 10; Spassky–Petrosian.

| 9 | 0–0 | |

Perhaps 9 0–0–0 is better.

9	...	h6
10	♗h4	♗e7
11	♖ae1	

On 11 f4 Black could play 11 ... ♕c5.

11	...	♘e5
12	♗b3	g5!
13	♗g3	♗d7
14	f4	gf
15	♗xf4	♕c7!

But not 15 ... 0–0–0 at once, because of a tactical trick which is typical of such positions: 16 ♘d5.

16	♘f3	0–0–0
17	♔h1	♖hg8
18	♗e3	♗c6

The light-squared bishop on c6 is the pride and joy of Black's position, and later it will perform excellently. But for the time being the white queen is going to invade on the weakened dark squares.

| 19 | ♕d4 | ♖g6 |

20	♖e2	♖dg8
21	♕a7	(26)

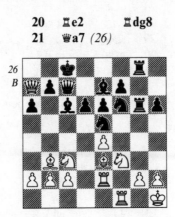

One gets the impression that White has the initiative, and that his queen is tying Black's forces down. But Black's position has a number of attractive features (doubled rooks on the half-open g-file, a bishop on c6 pointing along the diagonal towards White's king, a centralised knight on e5), and these rapidly become the decisive factors.

21	...	♘xe4
22	♗b6	♘xc3!! (27)

For the sake of opening the h1–a8 diagonal Black does not baulk at sacrificing his queen. White cannot refuse this gift: if now 23 ♖xe5 then possible are both 23 ... ♗xf3 and the quiet 23 ... ♕b8, and in the event of 23 ♘xe5 then 23 ... ♘xe2 24 ♘xg6 ♖xg6 is decisive.

23	♗xc7	♘xe2
24	♗b6	♖xg2
25	♗a4!!	(28)

An excellent defence. The threat is 26 ♕a8+ and 27 ♕xb7+.

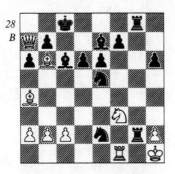

25	...	♖g1+!

The only way to get rid of the white pieces threatening Black's king.

26	♗xg1

26 ♖xg1 ♗xf3+ leads to mate.

26	...	♖xg1+
27	♕xg1	

Or 27 ♖xg1 ♗xf3+ 28 ♖g2, when Black's three pieces and two pawns are much stronger than the white queen.

27	...	♗xf3+!

The tempting 27 ... ♘xf3 would have been refuted by 28 ♗xc6 ♘fxg1 29 ♖xf7, when only White can have thoughts of winning.

28	♗xf3	♘xg1
29	♖c3+	♔d8
30	♔xg1	d5

The smoke has cleared. Black has two pawns for the exchange, menacing passed pawns in the centre and definite winning chances. Black turned his advantages into victory rather easily.

31	♖g3	♗g5
32	b4	b5
33	♗b3	f5
34	c3	♔e7
35	a4	f4

Now the white rook is effectively shut out of the game.

36	♖h3	♘c4
37	ab	ab
38	♔f2	♔d6
39	♔e2	e5

40	♗xc4	bc
41	♖h5	e4
42	h4	f3+
43	♔d1	♗f4
44	♖f5	

Black has a simple win: 44 ... ♗e5 45 ♔c2 ♔e6 46 ♖f8 ♗d6!
47 ♖e8+ ♗e7 48 ♔d2 d4! 49 cd c3+ 50 ♔xc3 f2.
White resigned.

Game No. 10
Spassky–Petrosian
18th game, World Ch. 1969

1	e4	c5
2	♘f3	d6
3	d4	cd
4	♘xd4	♘f6
5	♘c3	a6
6	♗g5	♘bd7

Petrosian had found this formation attractive for a long time,
and it seemed to him to be the most playable. But it has its
drawbacks: Black determines the position of his queen's knight
rather too early — in a number of variations it gets in the way of
the bishop on c8, and the white bishop manages to occupy the
a2–g8 diagonal, where it can be employed successfully in both
defence and attack.

7	♗c4	♕a5

On 7 ... e6, very unpleasant for Black is 8 ♗xe6!. Compelling
White to determine the position of his bishop on g5 by playing 7
... h6 had sad consequences in the game Tal–Bilek, Amsterdam
1964: 8 ♗xf6 ♘xf6 9 ♕e2 e6 10 0–0–0 ♕c7 11 f4 e5 12 ♘d5
♘xd5 13 ed ♗e7 14 fe de 15 ♘e6! with an irresistible attack for
White.

8	♕d2	h6

Here this move with the h-pawn is more expedient than on the
previous move: the queen is less active on d2 than on e2.

9	♗xf6	

An extremely common idea: White gives Black the advantage
of the two bishops, but thanks to his substantial lead in development he gets a fine attacking position.

9	...	♘xf6

10	0-0-0	e6
11	♖he1	

Bondarevsky considered that 11 ♗b3 is more accurate, since White's best continuation is still far from clear.

But the psychological effect of the move played is considerable: the black king begins to feel uneasy in the centre.

11	...	♗e7?!

The start of an incorrect plan. Analysis by Bondarevsky shows that castling long would have allowed Black to get a defensible position. On 11 ... ♗d7 12 f4 0-0-0 13 f5 Black has the counter 13 ... d5, and if 14 ed then 14 ... ef, when Black's position is satisfactory. True, on 13 ... d5 White is not obliged to reply 14 ed but can play 14 fe, and if 14 ... fe then 15 ed ed 16 ♘xd5, winning a pawn. But the point is that after 14 fe Black does not reply 14 ... fe? but 14 ... dc! 15 ed+ ♖xd7, when White cannot manage to exploit his lead in development. For example: 16 ♕e2 ♗b4 17 ♕xc4+ ♖c7, or 16 e5 ♘d5 17 ♘de2 ♗b4 18 ♕d4 ♖hd8! 19 ♕xc4+ ♔b8, and Black's game is quite in order.

12	f4	0-0
13	♗b3	♖e8

Foreseeing the need to defend the pawn on e6.

14	♔b1	♗f8 *(29)*

On 14 ... ♗d7 unpleasant would be 15 e5 de 16 fe ♘h7 17 ♘f5!, when Black's position is bad, since on 17 ... ♗c6 there follows 18 ♘xe7+ ♖xe7 19 ♘d5.

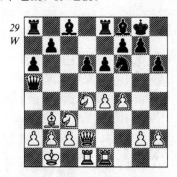

29
W

15	g4!

A classic storm after castling has taken place on opposite sides of the board. White has prepared for his offensive very successfully and now it is not easy for Black to defend. The lesser evil would have been 15 ... e5 16 ♘f5 ♗xf5 17 gf ef 18 ♘d5! ♕d8 19 ♕xf4 ♖e5.

	15	...	♘xg4
	16	♕g2	♘f6
	17	♖g1	♗d7
	18	f5	

With the threat 19 fe ♗xe6 (if 19 ... fe then 20 ♘f5) 20 ♘xe6 fe 21 ♕h3.

| | 18 | ... | ♔h8 |

After the f-file is opened up White's attack will prove irresistible. Therefore Black should have chosen 18 ... ef, when 19 ef b5 20 ♕g6 ♔h8 21 ♗xf7 b4 would have led to a hard struggle. Another possibility was 18 ... e5, not allowing lines to be opened. Attempts to refute this move by force would lead to unclear positions. For example: 19 ♕g6 ♔h8 20 ♕xf7 ♖e7 (but not 20 ... ed because of 21 ♘d5 ♘xe4 22 f6 g5 23 ♘e7). It is best for White to retreat the knight from d4 to e2, with an excellent position.

| | 19 | ♖df1 | ♕d8 |

Now, though, 19 ... e5 loses, in view of 20 ♘e6! fe 21 fe ♗xe6 22 ♖xf6 ♗xb3 23 ♖xf8+.

Black's best continuation was 19 ... ♕e5, although here too after 20 ♘f3 ♕f4 21 ♕h3 (threatening 22 ♘g5) White's attack is very strong.

| | 20 | fe | fe *(30)* |

Somewhat better was 20 ... ♗xe6. In this case White would play simply 21 ♘xe6 fe 22 ♘e2, with a very strong attack on the light squares.

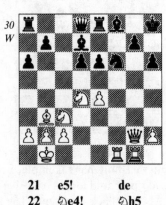

30
W

	21	e5!	de
	22	♘e4!	♘h5

The white knight on e4 cannot be captured, because of 23 ♖xf8+, and on 22 ... ed there follows 23 ♖xf6, with irresistible threats.

23   ♕g6!   ed *(31)*

Black cannot save the game with 23 ... ♘f4. After 24 ♖xf4 ef the quiet move 25 ♘f3 would be decisive in view of the threat 26 ♘g5 (with either knight). On 23 ... ♕b6 decisive is 24 ♖g5! ♗c6 25 ♘f6 ♘xf6 26 ♖xf6 (analysis by Geller).

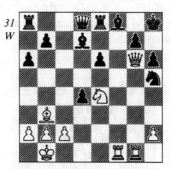

24   ♘g5!

On 24 ... hg there follows 25 ♕xh5+ ♔g8 26 ♕f7+ ♔h8 27 ♖f3 with inevitable mate.

Black resigned.

Game No. 11
Hübner–Visier
Las Palmas 1974

1	e4	c5
2	♘f3	e6
3	♘c3	♘c6
4	d4	cd
5	♘xd4	d6
6	♗e3	♘f6
7	♗c4	♗e7
8	♕e2	a6
9	0–0–0	♕c7
10	♗b3	0–0
11	♖hg1	

An alternative here is 11 g4 (see Game 12; Szmetan–G. Garcia and Game 37; Wahls–Hübner).

| 11 | ... | ♞a5 |

It is considered more sound to play 11 ... ♞d7 (see Game 42; Ivanovic–Larsen and Game 49; Brunner–Hübner).

12	g4	b5
13	g5	♞xb3+
14	ab	♞d7
15	♖g3	♝b7

An inaccuracy. The threats of thematic sacrifices of knights on d5 and f5 compel Black to be extremely attentive. Good was 15 ... ♖e8, defending the bishop on e7 and preparing to retreat it to f8, where it would cover the g7-square.

| 16 | f4 | b4 *(32)* |

Forcing White to sacrifice a piece. Here the rook on f8 was no longer able to leave its post, in view of the variation 16 ... ♖fc8 17 f5 b4 18 g6 bc 19 gf+ ♔xf7 20 ♖xg7+!, but worth considering was 16 ... ♞c5.

| 17 | ♞d5 | ed |
| 18 | ♞f5 | ♞c5 |

Here it was simply essential to play 18 ... ♖fe8, after which White would have had to make quite some effort to prove the correctness of his sacrifice. For example: 19 ♝d4 ♞e5! 20 ed ♝f8.

| 19 | ♝d4 | |

Underlining the weakness of the g7-square. Less good was the direct 19 ♕h5 ♖fc8 20 ♝xc5 dc 21 ♖h3 h6 22 ♞xh6+ gh 23 ♕xh6 ♕xf4+ 24 ♔b1 ♕e5 25 g6 ♕g7 26 gf+ ♔f8, when Black repels the attack.

| 19 | ... | ♞xe4 |

On 19 ... ♞e6 there could have followed 20 ed ♝xd5 21 ♝b6!,

regaining the piece.

20 ♘xg7 f6

This loses by force, but there was apparently no way to save the game. Black loses after 20 ... ♘xg3 21 hg f6 22 ♘f5 ♖f7 (22 ... ♖ae8 23 ♕e6+ ♚h8 24 gf) 23 ♘h6+ ♚g7 24 ♘xf7 ♚xf7 25 ♕h5+ ♚e6 26 ♖e1+ ♚d7 27 ♕f7, and the try 20 ... ♖fc8, with the threat of mate tying White's pieces down, would be repelled by 21 ♖h3 a5 22 ♘f5 ♗f8 (22 ... ♗a6 23 ♖xh7!) 23 ♚b1! (but not 23 ♖xh7 because of 23 ... ♕xc2+!).

21 gf ♘xg3 *(33)*

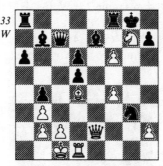

22 ♕g4! ♘e2+
23 ♚b1 ♗c8

On 23 ... h5 White would win with 24 ♕g5 ♗xf6 25 ♗xf6 ♚f7 26 f5 ♘f4 27 ♘e6!.

24 ♘f5+ ♚f7
25 ♕h5+ ♚e6
26 fe!

Threatening a piquant mate in one: 27 ef(♘) mate! On 26 ... ♖g8, decisive is 27 e8(♕)+ ♖xe8 28 ♘g7+.

26 ... ♗d7
27 ef(♘)+ Black resigned.

Game No. 12
Szmetan–G. Garcia
Torremolinos 1976

1	e4	c5
2	♘f3	e6
3	d4	cd
4	♘xd4	♘c6

5	♞c3	d6
6	♗e3	♞f6
7	♗c4	a6
8	♕e2	♗e7
9	0-0-0	♕c7
10	♗b3	0-0
11	g4	♞xd4
12	♖xd4	b5
13	g5	♞d7
14	♖g1	

14 f4 is considered in Game 37; Wahls–Hübner.

14	...	♞c5
15	e5!?	*(34)*

The idea behind this move is the immediate transfer of the white rook to the h-file.

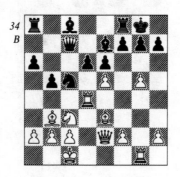

34
B

15	...	g6

Evidently more accurate was 15 ... d5 (not allowing a subsequent ♞c3–e4) or the immediate 15 ... ♞xb3+.

16	♖h4	♗b7
17	♖g3	♔g7
18	♗d4!	d5?

Of course, the preliminary 18 ... ♞xb3+ was essential, but now the bishop on b3 is very effective and comes into play at just the right time.

19	♗xd5!	♗xd5
20	♞xd5	ed
21	e6+	f6 *(35)*

Not 21 ... ♔g8, because of 22 ♖xh7. The impression is that White's attack has come to a dead-end. But White finds a brilliant

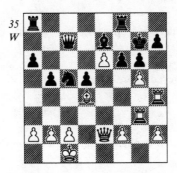

tactical continuation, allowing him to open up the position with great effect.

| 22 | ♕h5!! | ♘d3+ |
| 23 | ♔b1 | gh |

Alas, Black has to take the queen, but now the black king is put through the mincer.

| 24 | gf++ | ♔h8 |

No better was 24 ... ♔h6 25 ♗e3+ ♘f4 26 ♖xf4, when mate is inevitable.

| 25 | fe+ | |

Yet another unpleasant opening of a line.

25	...	♘e5
26	ef(♕)+	♖xf8
27	♖xh5	♖xf2
28	♗xf2	Black resigned.

Game No. 13
Anand–Ninov
Baguio City 1987

1	e4	c5
2	♘f3	e6
3	d4	cd
4	♘xd4	a6
5	♗d3	

Unlike 5 ♘c3, the continuation 5 ♗d3 retains the possibility for White to play c2–c4. Many players of Black consider the variation with 5 ♗d3 to be the most unpleasant reply to the Paulsen System and choose a different move order: 1 e4 c5 2 ♘f3 e6 3 d4 cd 4 ♘xd4 ♘c6.

| | 5 ... | ♗c5 |

A move introduced into practice by Polugayevsky.

| | 6 | ♘b3 |

The main continuation. The other possible moves, 6 c3 and 6 ♗e3, are encountered more rarely.

	6 ...	♗a7
	7 ♘c3	♘c6
	8 ♕e2	

White prepares to exchange dark-squared bishops by playing 9 ♗e3.

	8 ...	d6
	9 ♗e3	♗xe3
	10 ♕xe3	♘f6 *(36)*

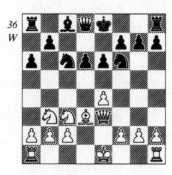

| | 11 | g4 |

This continuation (and also 11 0–0–0, see Game 14; Kengis–Nevednichy) leads to a sharp fight and poses serious problems for Black.

| | 11 ... | b5 |

Also possible is capturing the pawn: 11 ... ♘xg4 12 ♕g3 ♘f6 13 ♕xg7 ♖g8 14 ♕h6 ♗d7!, followed by 15 ... ♕e7 and 16 ... 0–0–0.

| | 12 0–0–0 | 0–0 |
| | 13 g5 | ♘e8 |

Another possibility was 13 ... ♘d7, and now White can either pressurise the pawn on d6 with 14 ♗e2 or attack Black's kingside with 14 f4, when after 14 ... ♕c7 we would transpose to Kengis–Nevednichy.

| | 14 f4 | b4 |
| | 15 ♘e2 | a5 |

16	♘bd4	♘xd4
17	♘xd4	♕b6?!

A loss of time. Black should have continued his pawn offensive with 17 ... a4.

| 18 | e5! |

A timely opening of the b1–h7 diagonal; the threat is the double attack 19 ♕e4.

18	...	♗b7
19	♖hf1	

White is preparing to break through with 20 f5.

19	...	de
20	fe	♖d8 *(37)*

Very careless. Black should have played 20 ... g6, although in this case White would exchange queens (21 ♘f5) with a big advantage.

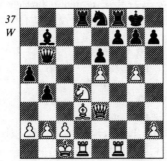

21	♗xh7+	♔xh7
22	g6+!	♔g8

The continuation 22 ... ♔xg6 23 ♕d3+ f5 (on 23 ... ♔h6 there would follow 24 ♕h3+) 24 ef+ also leads to a rout of Black's position.

23	♕h3	♘f6
24	ef	fg
25	fg	Black resigned.

On 25 ... ♔xg7 (not 25 ... ♖xf1 because of 26 ♕h8+), there would follow simply 26 ♘xe6+ ♔g8 27 ♖xf8+ ♖xf8 28 ♘xf8 ♔xf8 29 ♕h8+ ♔e7 (if 29 ... ♔f7 then 30 ♖f1+) 30 ♕g7+ ♔e8 31 ♖e1+ ♔d8 32 ♕f8+ ♔c7 33 ♖e7+.

Game No. 14
Kengis–Nevednichy
Moscow 1979

1	e4	c5
2	♘f3	e6
3	d4	cd
4	♘xd4	a6
5	♗d3	♗c5
6	♘b3	♗a7
7	♛e2	♘c6
8	♗e3	♗xe3

Worth considering is the continuation 8 ... d6, which was encountered in the game Timoshchenko–Vasyukov, Moscow 1981. There followed: 9 ♗xa7 ♖xa7 10 ♘c3 ♘f6 11 0–0 0–0 12 ♖ad1 b5 13 ♛e3 ♖c7 14 ♖d2 ♗b7 15 ♖fd1 ♘e5 16 a3 ♖xc3!? (an interesting exchange sacrifice requiring further investigation) 17 bc ♛c7 18 f3 ♖c8 19 ♖e1 h6 20 ♗f1 ♘fd7 21 ♛d4 d5 with complicated play.

9	♛xe3	♘f6
10	♘c3	d6
11	0–0–0	0–0
12	f4	♛c7
13	g4	

Alternatives here are 13 ♛h3 as in Game 38 (Bronstein–Suetin) and 13 ♖hg1; Game 57 (Spassky–Capelan).

13	...	b5

Black might do better to accept the sacrifice by playing 13 ... ♘xg4 (see Game 57; Spassky–Capelan).

14	g5	♘d7
15	f5!?	

Kengis rushes headlong into endless complications.

15	...	b4
16	♘e2	a5
17	♛h3	

Playing 17 ♘bd4 would not promise White much; after 17 ... ♘de5 (worse is 17 ... ♛b6 because of 18 fe fe 19 ♖hf1 ♖xf1 20 ♖xf1, with the threat of 21 ♖f8+!) 18 ♖hf1 ♗d7 Black has quite good prospects on the queenside.

17	...	ef?

In the spirit of this position was 17 ... ♘de5 followed by ...

♗c8–d7. For example: 18 f6 ♗d7 19 fg ♖fc8 and White's offensive comes to a dead-end, whereas Black develops a dangerous counterattack.

	18	ef	♘de5
	19	♘f4	a4
	20	♘d5	♕d8 *(38)*

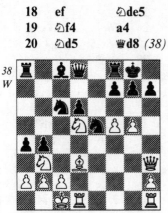

21   ♖hg1!

The prelude to a lovely combination.

21   ...   ♘xd3+?

Instead of this move Gipslis recommended 21 ... ab 22 ♘f6+ gf 23 ♕h6! ♘g6! 24 fg fg6 25 ♗xg6 ♖a7 26 gf hg!, when play is double-edged.

| | 22 | ♖xd3 | ♘e5 |
| | 23 | ♘f6+ | gf *(39)* |

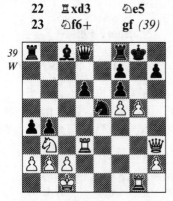

24   ♕h6!!

The point of White's idea. Now, as Kengis points out, Black cannot save the game after 24 ... ♔h8 25 ♖h3 ♗xf5 26 g6!!, as there is no defence against checkmate.

24   ...   ♘xd3+

25	♔b1!

But not 25 cd, in view of 25 ... ♔h8 26 g6 fg 27 fg ♕c7+! and
28 ... ♕g7.

25	...	fg
26	f6	♕xf6
27	♕xf6	g4
28	♕g5+	

As a result of his beautiful combination White has obtained an
advantage in material, and he now proceeded to turn this into
victory.

28	...	♔h8
29	♕f6+	♔g8
30	♘d4	♘e5
31	h3!	h5
32	♕g5+	♘g6
33	♕xh5	gh
34	♕d5	

A double attack: White threatens 35 ♕xa8 and 35 ♖xg6+.

34	...	♗e6
35	♘xe6	h2
36	♖xg6+	Black resigned.

On 36 ... fg there follows 37 ♘xf8+ ♔xf8 38 ♕xa8+.

Game No. 15
Short–Ehlvest
Rotterdam 1989

1	e4	c5
2	♘f3	d6
3	d4	cd
4	♘xd4	♘f6
5	♘c3	a6
6	♗e3	e6
7	f3	♘c6
8	g4	♗e7
9	♕d2	0–0
10	0–0–0	♘xd4

10 ... ♖b8 is considered in Game 54; Khalifman–Kasparov.

11	♗xd4	♘d7
12	h4	

White has adopted a formation which is characteristic of the fight against the 'Dragon'. His attack looks extremely menacing, but there are no weaknesses in Black's position.

	12	...	b5
	13	g5	♖b8
	14	♗h3?!	

More accurate was 14 ♔b1.

| | 14 | ... | ♕c7 *(40)* |

A better reaction would have been 14 ... ♘e5.

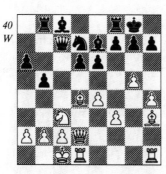

15 g6?!

The signal for a storm: this is a typical pawn sacrifice in such positions, with the aim of opening lines.

	15	...	hg
	16	h5	♘e5!

White's attack would become unstoppable in the event of 16 ... b4?, as there would follow: 17 ♘d5 ed 18 hg (with the terrible threat of 19 ♗xd7, ♖h8+ and ♕h6+) 18 ... fg 19 ♗e6+ ♖f7 20 ♖h8+ ♔xf7 21 ♗xf7 and Black is defenceless. In the event of 16 ... g5 unpleasant is 17 h6 gh 18 ♗g4. Also bad for Black is 16 ... gh, in view of 17 ♖dg1 ♗f6 18 ♗xf6 ♘xf6 19 ♖xg7+! ♔xg7 20 ♕g5+.

| | 17 | hg | fg |

Black decided against playing 17 ... ♘xf3, evidently fearing a spectacular variation: 18 ♗xe6?! ♘xd2? 19 ♖h7!! ♘b3+ 20 ♔b1 (but not 21 ab ♗g5+ and 22 ... ♗h6) 20 ... ♘xd4 21 ♖dh1.

But Black has a refutation: 18 ... ♗g5! 19 ♖h7 ♗xd2+ 20 ♔b1 (or 20 ♖xd2 fe) 20 ... ♘xd4 21 ♖dh1 ♗h6. White also achieves nothing with 18 ♕g2 fg 19 ♕xg6, because of 19 ... ♘xd4 20 ♖xd4 ♗f6.

| | 18 | ♗g4 | b4 |

It would be bad to play 18 ... ♘xf3, because of 19 ♖h8+! ♔xh8 20 ♕h6+.

	19	♗xe5	de
	20	♘e2	♖b6
	21	♔b1	a5?

Black should have interpolated the moves 21 ... ♖d8 and 22 ... ♖xd1+.

| | 22 | ♘c1 | ♖d8 |
| | 23 | ♘d3 | a4?! |

23 ... ♗a6 looks stronger.

| | 24 | ♕h2 | ♗f6 (41) |

White would also get a very strong attack after 24 ... b3 25 cb ab 26 ♖c1 ♕a7 27 a3 ♖xd3 28 ♖xc8+ ♔f7 29 f4.

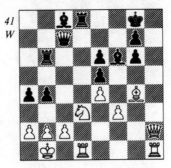

| | 25 | f4 | ef |

The continuation 25 ... b3 26 cb ab 27 fe ♕xc2+ 28 ♕xc2 bc 29 ♔xc2 would not promise anything good for Black.

| | 26 | e5! | ♗g5 |
| | 27 | ♕h7+ | ♔f7 (42) |

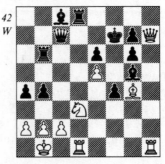

| | 28 | ♗h5! |

Finally destroying Black's bastions.

28	...	gh
29	♕xh5+	♚g8
30	♖dg1!	

Not wasting time in taking the bishop, White brings another rook into the attack and quickly brings the game to an end.

30	...	♝b7
31	♕h7+	♚f8
32	♖xg5	♕f7
33	♖h4	♖d4
34	♖hg4	g6
35	♕h8+	♕g8
36	♕h4	b3

On 36 ... ♚f7 decisive is 37 ♖h5!.

37	♖xg6	bc+
38	♚c1	Black resigned.

3 Storming a Queenside Castled Position after Castling on Opposite Sides

On playing through the games in Chapter Two the reader might have the impression that after castling has taken place on opposite sides the king situated on the kingside usually has a tough time. But the converse can also be true: the king which remains on the kingside turns out to be completely safe, whereas his counterpart, which has castled on the queenside, will have a ferocious storm to repel. In Sicilian games a queenside castled position can turn out to be highly vulnerable, partly due to the half-open c-file.

When supported by pieces, a pawn offensive against a queenside castled position is highly effective if the attacking side can succeed in totally neutralising his opponent's attack on the opposite wing (see the game Wedberg–Kozul below).

For this chapter several other games have been selected in which a storm of the queenside castled position is triumphant, various tactical methods being employed in the process.

Wedberg–Kozul
Novi Sad Ol. 1990

The position in diagram 43 arose after White's 20th move in one of the variations of the Sozin Attack. Neither pawn offensive looks particularly menacing but, all the same, Black's position makes the better impression, thanks to the secure position of his king.

Having a lead in development, Black is first to take decisive action.

20	...	♖ac8
21	♔b1	c4

More accurate was 21 ... ♖c6! followed by 22 ... ♖fc8 and 23 ... c4.

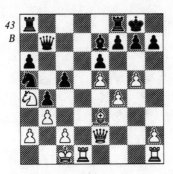

22	♗b6!	cb
23	ab?	

White has overlooked an unpleasant move by the black knight. The game would have been level after 23 cb ♗d8 24 ♗xa5 ♗xa5 25 ♖c1.

23	...	♘c4!
24	bc	♕c6
25	♘b2	

Alas, the pawn on c2 hinders White's defence of his knight (he cannot play 25 ♕c2).

25	...	♕xb6
26	♖d7	♗c5
27	♖hd1	b3!

A very important move, thanks to which some very important lines are opened up.

28	cb	♕xb3
29	♖d3	♕b6
30	♖h3	♖b8
31	♖d2	g6!

Not forgetting about prophylactic measures as well!

32	♕e1	

With a little trap: 32 ... ♗b4 33 ♕h4 h5 34 gh ♔h7 35 ♕f6.

32	...	♗e7!
33	♕c1	

Now on 33 ♕h4 Black would play 33 ... h5.

33	...	♖b7
34	♖c2	♖c8
35	♖d3	♗c5

Black has deployed his pieces quite superbly, and tactics against the defenceless white king are now inevitable.

36	♕d2	♖cb8
37	♔c1	♗b4
38	♕e3	♕a5
39	♔d1	♗c5
40	♕d2	♕a1+
41	♕c1	♕a2!

White resigned.

Game No. 16
Smyslov–Romanishin
USSR Ch., Moscow 1976

1	e4	c5
2	♘c3	♘c6
3	g3	g6
4	♗g2	♗g7
5	d3	d6
6	♘h3	

More common continuations are 6 ♘ge2, 6 ♗e3, and 6 f4.

6	...	h5

Romanishin opts for active play, probably hoping by such means to cast doubt on the wisdom of the flank development of the white knight.

7	f4	♗g4
8	♕d2	♘d4
9	♘g1!	

By returning the knight to its initial position, White not only covers the f3-square but also prepares to play h2–h3, driving away the enemy bishop and obtaining an advantage.

9	...	♕d7?!

It looks more natural to play 9 ... ♕a5, but developing the queen to d7 is associated with a very original plan of castling long. Play becomes very sharp.

10	h3	♗e6
11	♘ce2	h4
12	g4	f5
13	ef	

White handles the position quite simply: first he opens the diagonal for his light-squared bishop, and then by playing g4–g5 he slows down Black's kingside development.

13	...	gf
14	g5	0-0-0
15	♘xd4	cd
16	♘e2	♗f7

Without withdrawing the bishop Black cannot develop his knight.

17	c3	dc
18	bc	♔b8
19	♖b1	d5
20	0-0	

It also looked quite good to play 20 d4, with the possible continuation 20 ... e6 21 ♗a3, followed by the transfer of the knight via c1 to b3. In the Sicilian it is quite unusual to see White castle kingside and Black queenside!

20	...	e5
21	fe	♗xe5
22	d4	♗c7
23	c4	♘e7
24	c5	

Worth considering was 24 ♕b2, provoking 24 ... b6. But White intends to transfer his queen to b4.

24	...	♖dg8
25	♕b4	♗d8 *(44)*

26 ♖f3!

The transfer of the rook along the third rank promises to strengthen the attack against the black king with decisive effect. This decision required correct calculation, since it turns out that Black has active counterplay involving an attack on the pawn at g5.

| 26 | ... | ♘c6 |

Tempting was 26 ... ♗h5, but in this case, as Smyslov writes, there could have followed 27 ♖fb3! ♗xe2 28 ♕xb7+ ♕xb7 29 ♖xb7+ ♔c8 30 ♗f4 with a very strong attack. For example: 30 ... ♗c4 31 ♖xe7 ♗xe7 32 c6 and mate is unavoidable. Black cannot save the game with 30 ... ♖g6, because of 31 ♖xa7 ♘c6 32 ♖a8+ ♔d7 33 ♗xd5.

27	♕b5	♗h5
28	♖fb3	♖g7
29	♘f4	

White does not give his opponent any respite. On 29 ... ♘xd4, there would have followed 30 ♕xd7 ♖xd7 31 ♗b2! ♘xb3 32 ♗xh8 ♘d2 33 ♘xh5 ♘xb1 34 g6, and the g-pawn promotes.

| 29 | ... | ♗xg5 |
| 30 | ♘xh5 | ♖xh5 *(45)* |

45
W

| 31 | ♕e2! | |

A subtle retreat. While attacking the rook on h5 White opens a path for his rooks to strike at b7.

| 31 | ... | ♗xc1 |

On 31 ... ♖h8 there would have followed 32 ♗xg5 ♖xg5 33 ♖xb7+ ♕xb7 34 ♖xb7+ ♔xb7 35 ♔h2 ♖d8 36 ♕e6! f4 37 ♕f7+ ♔c8 38 ♕f6 and White wins.

| 32 | ♖xb7+ | ♕xb7 *(46)* |
| 33 | ♕e8+! | |

Essential accuracy. After this check Black will be forced to capture the rook on b7 with his king.

33	...	♔c7
34	♖xb7+	♔xb7
35	♕xh5	♘xd4

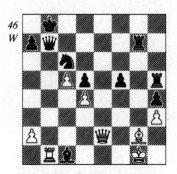

36	♔f1	♗e3
37	♕h8	♖d7
38	♕e8	Black resigned.

Game No. 17
Epishin–Dvoiris
USSR Ch., Leningrad 1990

1	e4	c5
2	♘f3	d6
3	♗b5+	♘c6

An equal game results after 3 ... ♗d7 4 ♗xd7+ ♕xd7 5 0–0 ♘f6 6 ♖e1 e6 7 c3 ♘c6 8 d4 cd 9 cd d5! 10 e5 ♘e4!, or 5 d4 cd 6 ♘xd4 ♘f6 7 ♘c3 g6 8 0–0 ♗g7 9 ♗e3 0–0 10 f4 ♖e8 11 ♕f3 a6 12 ♖ad1.

4	d4	

Black gets a satisfactory game in the event of 4 0–0 ♗g4, see Game 25; Ambroz–Rausis.

4	...	cd
5	♕xd4	♗d7
6	♗xc6	♗xc6
7	♘c3	♘f6
8	♗g5	e6
9	0–0–0	♗e7
10	♖he1	0–0

Black has played the opening quietly, and his two bishops guarantee him good prospects.

11	♕d2	♕a5
12	♔b1	♕a6

The threat was 13 ♘d5.

13	♘d4	♖fc8
14	f3	b5
15	g4	b4
16	♘ce2	♗e8
17	♘g3	h6?!

Black has an excellent position, and there was absolutely no need to weaken his king's pawn cover; 17 ... ♖c5 did not look bad.

| 18 | ♗e3 | ♘d7 *(47)* |

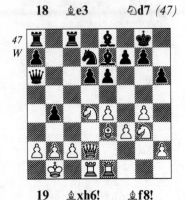

47
W

| 19 | ♗xh6! | ♗f8! |

In the event of 19 ... gh 20 ♕xh6, followed by the knights jumping in, White's attack would have been quite menacing.

| 20 | ♗g5? | |

An inaccuracy: stronger was 20 ♗e3 or 20 ♘h5 gh 21 g5.

| 20 | ... | ♘e5 |
| 21 | ♘h5 | ♖c5! |

A very strong move: Black takes control of the fifth rank, putting an end to all of White's threats and transferring his rook to the a-file. The threat is 22 ... ♘c4.

22	b3	♖a5
23	♕e2 *(48)*	
23	...	♗b5!

With the help of an interference move Black avoids the exchange of queens.

24	♘xb5	♖xa2
25	♔c1	♖c8
26	♘d4	♖axc2+!

The decisive blow: Black destroys the white king's pawn cover

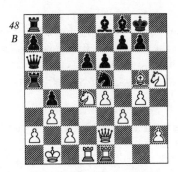

and clears a path for his queen, which now comes into play with tremendous effect.

27	♘xc2	♛a1+
28	♔d2	♛c3+
29	♔c1	♘xf3 *(49)*

The threat is 30 ... ♛a1 mate.

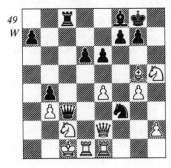

30	♔b1	♛xb3+
31	♔c1	♛a2!

Mate is inevitable. White resigned.

Game No. 18
Gavrikov–Tukmakov
Yerevan 1982

1	e4	c5
2	♘f3	d6
3	d4	cd
4	♘xd4	♘f6
5	♘c3	♘c6
6	♗g5	e6

7	♕d2	a6

Black prevents possible attempts by White to take advantage of the weakness of the d6-square. But he is very late in developing his kingside, and this allows White to create tactical complications in a number of variations by exploiting the insecure position of the black king.

8	0-0-0	h6

This system, devised by Aronin, leads to a sharp and tense struggle with chances for both sides.

Playable for Black is 8 ... ♗d7, with the possible continuation 9 f4 h6 10 ♗h4 ♘xe4 11 ♕e1 ♘f6 12 ♘f5 ♕a5 13 ♘xd6+ ♗xd6 14 ♖xd6 0-0-0.

9	♗f4

The double-edged continuation 9 ♗h4 leads to complicated play, as now the tempting 9 ... ♘xe4 leads after 10 ♕f4 g5 11 ♕xe4 gh 12 ♘xc6 bc 13 ♕xc6+ ♗d7 14 ♕f3 ♖b8 15 ♗c4 to a position where Black has definite problems, in view of the unfortunate position of his king.

Also possible is 9 ♗e3, since it is not good for Black to play 9 ... ♘g4 10 ♘xc6 bc 11 ♗c5! (Smyslov–Botvinnik, 2nd game, World Ch., Moscow 1957), but Black gets an entirely acceptable game after 9 ... ♘xd4 followed by 10 ... b5.

9	...	♗d7
10	♘xc6	

The exchange of knights alleviates Black's defence; preferable was 10 ♗g3, after which 10 ... ♖c8 would be worth considering, in order on 11 ♘xc6 to have the reply 11 ... ♖xc6.

10	...	♗xc6
11	♕e1	

Tal's recommendation, this move enters into several plans. White threatens not only 12 e5 or 12 ♗xd6 ♗xd6 13 e5, but also 12 ♘d5 in some lines.

Interesting play arises after 11 f3 d5 12 ♕e1 ♗b4 13 a3 ♗a5! (after 13 ... ♗xc3 14 ♕xc3 White has a clear advantage) 14 ed (stronger is 14 b4! ♗b6 15 ed ♗xd5 16 ♗e5) 14 ... ♘xd5 15 b4 ♘xf4! 16 ♖xd8+ ♗xd8 and, thanks to White's weakened queenside, Black has sufficient positional compensation for the loss of his queen (Kostro–Simagin, Varna 1966).

11	...	♕a5
12	♗c4!	♗e7!

Now 13 ♗xd6 ♗xd6 14 ♖xd6 is not possible, in view of 14
... ♕c5!. Nor is White promised anything by 13 ♘d5 ♕xe1 14
♘xf6+ ♗xf6! 15 ♖hxe1 ♗g5! 16 ♗xg5 hg.

	13	f3	b5
	14	♗b3	♕c7
	15	♘e2	

White begins to play superficially and passively, as a result of
which he gets into difficulties. It looks more natural to continue
15 e5 de 16 ♗xe5 ♕b7 17 ♗xf6 ♗xf6 18 ♘d5.

	15	...	0-0
	16	g4	a5
	17	a3?	

This move is a serious error. Essential was 17 ♘d4 ♗d7 (17
... a4 18 ♗xe6) 18 e5 de 19 ♗xe5, although after 19 ... ♕b7
Black's position is to be preferred.

	17	...	♖fc8
	18	♔b1	

Now 18 ♘d4 would have come too late: 18 ... e5 19 ♘xc6
♕xc6 with 20 ... a4 to follow.

	18	...	a4

Playing 18 ... b4 would have allowed White to close the position
on the queenside with 19 a4.

	19	♗a2 *(50)*	

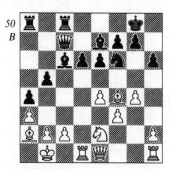

	19	...	b4!

The start of a decisive offensive.

	20	ab	

The continuation 20 ♕xb4 e5 21 ♗g3 ♗xe4 22 fe ♕xc2+ 23
♔a1 ♕xe2 would have given Black, in addition to his attack, an
advantage in material.

20	...	♗xe4!
21	fe	♕xc2+
22	♔a1	a3
23	♖b1	♕xe4

Much weaker was 23 ... ♘xe4 24 ♘d4 ♕d3 25 ♕e3.

24	♗d2	♘d5
25	♘c1	

As Tukmakov observes in his annotations to this game, various combinational ideas are in the air. One of them is 25 ♘c3 ab+! 26 ♔xb2 (26 ♖xb2 ♕xe1+ 27 ♖xe1+ ♘xc3) 26 ... ♘xc3 27 ♗xc3 ♖xa2+ 28 ♔xa2 ♕c2+ and 29 ... ♖a8 mate.

25	...	♕xe1

Black exchanges queens, but this does not weaken his attack.

26	♖xe1	♗f6
27	♖d1 *(51)*	

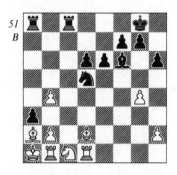

51
B

27	...	♖c2
28	♘d3	♘b6
29	♗c1	

Forced. It would be bad to play 29 ♗c3, because of 29 ... ♖xc3.

29	...	♘c4
30	b5 *(52)*	

An attempt by White to free himself somehow, but now comes a problem-like finish. White could only have continued his resistance by playing 30 ♖f1, with the threat of 31 ♖xf6. But in this case the variation 30 ... ab+ 31 ♖xb2 (it would be quite bad to play 31 ♗xb2 ♘d2, or 31 ♘xb2 ♖c3 32 ♘xc4 ♖ca3+ 33 ♖b2 ♖xa2+ 34 ♔b1 ♖a1+ 35 ♔c2 ♖c8) 31 ... ♘xb2 32 ♗xb2 ♗xb2+ 33 ♘xb2 ♖xh2 would not offer White much hope.

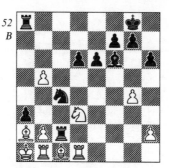

52
B

| 30 | ... | ♘a5!! |

White resigned.

There is no satisfactory defence against the threat 31 ... ♘b3+ 32 ♗xb3 ab mate. For example: 31 ♗d5 ♘b3+! 32 ♔a2 ♘xc1+ and then 33 ... ab+, eliminating white pieces one after another.

Game No. 19

Pruss–Blekhtsin

Dortmund 1991

1	e4	c5
2	♘f3	♘c6
3	d4	cd
4	♘xd4	♘f6
5	♘c3	d6
6	f3	e5
7	♘b3	♗e7
8	♗e3	0–0
9	♕d2	a6
10	0–0–0	

10 g4 would have set Black greater problems.

10	...	b5
11	♘d5	♘xd5
12	ed	♘b8
13	g4	a5!?
14	♔b1	

Now White gets an inferior position without any compensation.

Worth considering was 14 ♗xb5, when after 14 ... a4 15 ♘a1 ♘d7 16 c4 Black would have to work quite hard to develop his initiative.

14	...	b4
15	♘c1	♘d7
16	♗b5	♘b6
17	♕g2	♗a6
18	♗xa6	♖xa6
19	♘e2	♘c4
20	♗c1	a4
21	h4	♕b6
22	♖d3	(53)

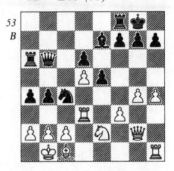

In this position Black has many tactical possibilities, but he preferred to increase his attacking potential.

22	...	e4!
23	fe	♗f6
24	♖f1	♗e5

The hasty 24 ... ♘a3+ could have led after 25 ♖xa3 ba 26 ♖xf6 to unclear complications.

25	b3	ab
26	cb	(54)

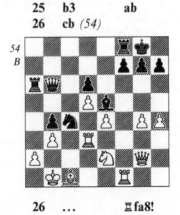

26	...	♖fa8!

27	♕f3	♕a7
28	bc	♖xa2
29	♘d4!	

The threat was 28 ... ♖b2+ 29 ♗xb2 ♕a2+ with mate.

29	...	♗xd4

Black should not have exchanged his strong bishop. More accurate was 29 ... ♖g2!.

30	♖xd4	♖h2
31	♕xf7+	

There is no other defence against mate.

31	...	♕xf7
32	♖xf7	♔xf7
33	h5	b3
34	♖d3	♖b8
35	♖f3+	

Worth considering was the immediate 35 ♗f4.

35	...	♔g8
36	♖f1	b2
37	♗f4	♖f8!

A decisive pin.

38	♗xh2	♖xf1+
39	♔xb2	♖f2+
40	♔c3	♖xh2

White resigned.

Game No. 20
Lukin–Kupreichik
Daugavpils 1989

1	e4	c5
2	♘f3	d6
3	d4	cd
4	♘xd4	♘f6
5	♘c3	a6
6	♗e3	e6
7	♗e2	♕c7
8	a4	b6
9	f4	♗b7
10	♗f3	♘bd7
11	♕e2	♘c5
12	♗f2	

White threatens 13 e5.

| | 12 | ... | e5 |
| | 13 | ♘f5 | |

More accurate was 13 fe de 14 ♘f5.

| | 13 | ... | g6 |

It would be bad to play 13 ... ef, because of 14 ♘d5.

| | 14 | ♗h4 *(55)* |

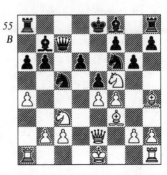

| | 14 | ... | ♘cd7 |

It would be bad to play 14 ... ♘fxe4 15 ♘xe4 ♘xe4 (15 ... gf 16 ♘f6+) 16 ♗xe4 ♗xe4 17 ♕xe4, since Black's rook on a8 is hanging.

| | 15 | ♘e3 | ♗e7 |
| | 16 | fe | |

Worth considering was 16 f5, when Black has no obvious counterplay.

| | 16 | ... | de |

Play would be unclear after 16 ... ♘xe5 17 ♗xf6 ♗xf6 18 ♘ed5 ♕d8 19 ♕f2 ♗g7.

| | 17 | 0-0-0 | 0-0 |
| | 18 | ♘ed5 | ♗xd5 |

Of course, Black cannot play 18 ... ♘xd5? because of 19 ♘xd5 ♗xd5 20 ♗xe7 ♖fe8 21 ed ♖xe7 22 d6.

	19	ed	♗d6
	20	g4 *(56)*	
	20	...	b5!

Black takes advantage of the weakening of White's castled position.

| | 21 | g5 | ba!? |

An ingenious piece sacrifice, but stronger was 21 ... b4! 22 gf

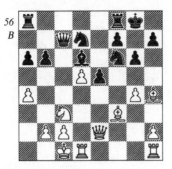

bc, or 22 ♘b1 ♘c5 23 ♘d2 ♘fd7.

22	gf	a3
23	♘e4	♕a5

Black threatens 24 ... a2, and now White should have played 24 b3! a2 25 ♔b2, with hopes of saving the game.

24	c3? *(57)*	

White overlooks another tactical trick.

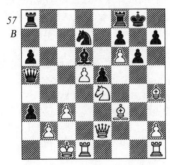

24	...	♖fb8!
25	♘xd6	

It would not help to play 25 b4, because of 25 ... ♗xb4!.

25	...	♖xb2
26	♕xb2	ab+
27	♔d2	

On 27 ♔c2 unpleasant is 27 ... ♕a4+; if 27 ♔xb2 then 27 ... ♖b8+ 28 ♔c1 ♕a2 is decisive.

27	...	♖b8
28	♖b1	e4!

Vacating a square for the knight, which comes into play with decisive effect.

29	♘xe4	♘e5
30	♗g2	♕xd5+
31	♔e2	♕d3+

White resigned.

After 32 ♔f2 ♘g4+ White loses the rook on b1.

Game No. 21
Campora–Yudasin
Moscow 1989

1	e4	c5
2	♘f3	d6
3	d4	cd
4	♘xd4	♘f6
5	♘c3	a6
6	♗e3	e6

Black transposes to the Scheveningen System. The most testing continuation is 6 ... e5, although also in this case White retains the possibility of choosing a system involving castling queenside. For example, 7 ♘b3 ♗e7 8 ♕d2 ♗e6 9 f3 ♘bd7 10 0–0–0 b5 11 g4 0–0 12 g5 ♘h5 13 ♖g1 with sharp play.

7 ♕d2

In this situation d2 is not the best square for the queen.

White's pieces appear to be placed better after 7 f4 b5 8 ♕f3 ♗b7 9 a3 ♘bd7 10 ♗d3. Also possible is 7 f3 b5 8 g4 (not wasting time in playing 8 ♕d2) 8 ... h6 9 h4 b4 10 ♘ce2 e5 11 ♘b3 d5 12 ♘g3 d4 13 ♗f2 ♗e6 14 ♗d3 h5 15 g5 ♘fd7 16 f4 ♗g4 17 ♗e2 ef 18 ♘xh5 when White has the initiative (Short–Ribli, Barcelona 1989).

Also worth considering is 7 a4 b6 8 a5!?, and now on 8 ... b5 (stronger is 8 ... ba) there follows 9 ♘dxb5! ab 10 ♗b6 ♕e7 11 ♗xb5+ ♘fd7 12 ♕d3 ♗b7 13 0–0 with a big advantage to White. In Sukhanov–Nikolenko, telephone game 1988, Black played 13 ... ♘c6 and White achieved a spectacular victory: 14 a6! ♘xb6 15 ♘d5! ed 16 ab ♕xb7 17 ed ♘xd5 18 ♕xd5 etc.

7	...	b5
8	f3	♗b7
9	0–0–0	♘bd7
10	g4	♘b6

The idea behind this move consists in vacating the d7-square for the king's knight and at the same time taking control of the

squares c4 and d5. Another possibility was 10 ... h6, when after
11 ♗d3 Black gets quite a good game by continuing 11 ... ♘e5
12 ♖he1 ♘fd7 13 f4 ♘g4 14 ♗g1 e5, or 11 ... b4 12 ♘ce2 d5 13
ed ♘xd5 14 ♘f4 ♕a5.

11	♕f2	♘fd7
12	♗d3	♖c8
13	h4	*(58)*

In the game T. Horvath–Vogt, Eger 1987, White played 13
♘ce2, and got a strong attack after 13 ... ♕c7 14 ♔b1 d5 15
♘g3 ♘c4? (better was 15 ... ♗e7) 16 ♗xc4 ♕xc4 17 ♘b3 ♕c7
18 ed ♗xd5 19 ♖xd5! ed 20 ♖e1 ♔d8 21 ♘f5.

Also worth considering is the immediate 13 ♔b1.

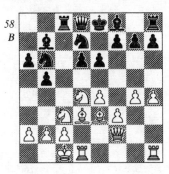

| 13 | ... | ♖xc3!? |

An exchange sacrifice, typical of many variations of the Sicilian
Defence, which abruptly changes the nature of the game.

14	bc	♕c7
15	♘e2	d5
16	e5	♘a4
17	f4	b4!

Black does not wish to lose time on the natural capture of a
pawn with 17 ... ♘xc3, as there would follow 18 ♘xc3 ♕xc3 19
♗d4, and instead brings his king's bishop into the game.

18	cb	♗xb4
19	♗d4	0–0
20	c3	♘dc5
21	♗c2	♘e4
22	♗xe4	de
23	♖h3	♕c4

Most of Black's pieces are in the immediate vicinity of the white king, and Black's threats are very unpleasant.

24	♔d2	♗a5

Black would achieve nothing by playing 24 ... ♕xa2+ 25 ♔e1 ♗a5 because of 26 ♘c1, when his attack is stifled.

25	♖a1	♖d8
26	♔e1	♗c6!

The bishop is being transferred to the f1–a6 diagonal.

27	♔f1	♗b5
28	♖b1	♗xc3
29	♖xb5!?	*(59)*

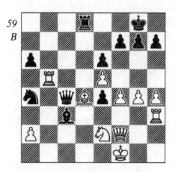

Now after 29 ... ♗xd4 White would have a chance, thanks to the weakness of Black's back rank: 30 ♕xd4! ♕xd4 31 ♘xd4 ab 32 ♘xb5.

29	...	ab!
30	♗xc3	♖d3!

This is the point of Black's idea: the rook on h3 is enticed onto a square where it can be taken by the pawn on e4.

31	♖xd3	ed
32	♗d2	de+
33	♕xe2	♕d5

After these very interesting complications the game has reached an ending which is difficult for White. Regrettably, pawns cannot move backwards!

34	♕g2	♕d3+
35	♔e1	h6
36	g5	h5
37	♕b7	♕b1+
38	♔e2	♕xa2

Now White cannot play 39 ♕xb5 because of 39 ... ♘c3+.

39	♕a8+	♚h7
40	♕e4+	g6
41	♕b4	♕c2
42	♕f8	♘c3+

It becomes clear that White will lose his bishop with check: 43 ♚f1 ♕d1+ 44 ♗e1 ♕e2+, or 43 ♚e3 ♕e4+ 44 ♚f2 ♕e2+ 45 ♚g1 (45 ♚g3 ♘e4+ 46 ♚h3 ♕f3+ leads to mate) 45 ... ♕d1+, and so he ends his resistance.

White resigned.

4 Storming a King Stuck in the Centre

It has long been known that a king stuck in the centre is an excellent target, but nevertheless this axiomatic notion is regularly subjected to practical examination. In a number of variations of the Sicilian Defence Black quite intentionally remains behind in development. He makes many pawn moves (d6, e6, a6, b5), does not rush to castle, leaving himself the option of sheltering his king on either the kingside or the queenside, and he often begins active play without having managed to castle at all. Exploiting these circumstances requires a considerable degree of tactical subtlety and, most of all, forceful play.

In order to keep the king in the centre and demolish its protective cover, piece sacrifices are sometimes employed, many of which are quite typical and crop up again and again. For example, capturing a black pawn on b5 or e6 with a knight or a bishop, and the manoeuvres ♘c3–d5 or ♘d4–f5, by means of which a white knight is sacrificed in order to open lines. Interesting in this respect are the games Urzica–Ungureanu and Tolnai–Tompa (see below).

Not just Black but also White sometimes sins by allowing his king to become stuck in the centre. This usually happens when he resolves to storm his opponent without wishing to waste time on castling (see the game Lutikov–Taimanov below).

Urzica–Ungureanu
Romania 1976

Diagram 60 is one of the key positions in the Polugayevsky System. Black's position has some positive aspects — in particular, his good pawn structure, pressure along the open and half-open files and the possibility of winning White's central pawn.

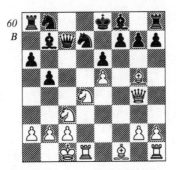

Nevertheless, Black's lack of development and the insecure position of his king are often the cause of disaster, and sacrifice of white pieces on b5 or e6 are frequently encountered.

In this game there followed:

| 12 | ... | h6? |

At first sight this is a logical move, asking the white bishop to leave the h4–d8 diagonal, but White's position is ripe for tactics.

| 13 | ♘xe6! | ♕xe5 |
| 14 | ♘c7+! | |

Deflection of the queen from the e-file.

| 14 | ... | ♕xc7 |
| 15 | ♕e2+ | Black resigned. |

On 15 ... ♘e5 there follows 16 ♕xe5+! ♕xe5 17 ♖d8 mate.

Tolnai–Tompa
Hungary 1990

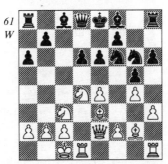

Black has chosen an active way to oppose the Panov–Keres Attack and seems to have built quite sound fortifications. But he has lost too much time and his king has got hopelessly stuck in the centre. White opens the central e-file (and at the same time the h1–a8 diagonal).

12	♘f5!	ef
13	ef	♘e5
14	f4	gf
15	♗xf4	♛c7
16	♖he1	♗e7
17	♗f3!	

Intending to launch a decisive pawn storm: 18 h4 and 19 g5.

17	...	♗d7
18	♗xb7!	

This time a deflection sacrifice of a piece.

18	...	♛xb7
19	♗xe5	0–0

Bad for Black would be 19 ... de 20 ♛xe5, when not only the bishop on e7 is pinned but also the knight on f6. Still, the black king has managed to castle, but it is too late.

20	♗d4	♖fe8
21	♛d2!	♘h7
22	♖xe7!	

White gets rid of his opponent's dark-squared bishop and carries out a decisive mating attack.

22	...	♖xe7
23	f6	♖b8
24	♛xh6	♛xb2+
25	♔d2	♘xf6
26	♗xf6	Black resigned.

Lutikov–Taimanov
USSR Ch., Moscow 1969

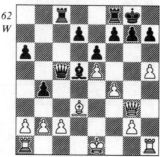

62
W

In this exceptionally hard-fought game White opposed the Paulsen System in a very original way and built up an attack against the enemy king. Nevertheless the insecure position of the white king gives Black excellent possibilities for launching a counter-attack.

25 ♖h4!

Demonstrating the most serious intentions.

25 ... ♛g1+!

At first sight this is a serious mistake: after 26 ♔d2 ♛xa1 27 ♖g4 Black cannot defend against the mating threats, but the purpose of this move is quite different — to deprive White of the opportunity to castle and to entice the king onto d2.

26 ♔d2 ♛d4
27 f5 ♖xc2+!

The start of a superb combination, involving the destruction of the white king's pawn cover and its enticement to a position where it can be attacked.

28 ♔xc2 b3+!
29 ♔d1

On 29 ab there could follow 29 ... ♗xb3+!, when it is bad to play 30 ♔xb3 because of 30 ... ♖b8+.

29 ... ♛g1+
30 ♛e1 ♛xg2

Black is a whole rook down, but his attack is very strong.

31 ♛f1 ♗f3+
32 ♔e1 ♛xb2
33 ♖b1 ♛xe5+
34 ♔f2 ba
35 ♖e1 ♛f6
36 ♔g3 ♗g2!

If White captures the bishop he loses one of his rooks: 37 ♔xg2 ♛xh4, or 37 ♛xg2 a1(♛).

37 ♛g1 ef

Now Black has six (!) pawns for the rook, and his attack continues.

38 ♛d4 ♛g5+
39 ♔h2 ♗e4
40 ♖hxe4 fe
41 ♛xe4 ♛xh5+

White resigned.

Game No. 22
Kholmov–Keres
USSR Ch., Tbilisi 1959

1	e4	c5
2	♘f3	♘c6
3	♗b5	♘f6
4	e5	♘g4
5	♗xc6	dc
6	0–0	g6
7	♖e1	♗g7
8	h3	♘h6
9	♘c3	b6?

This allows White to begin a deeply calculated combinational attack. Black should have preferred 9 ... 0–0, as Kholmov points out in his annotations to this game.

10	d4!	cd
11	♘xd4	c5 *(63)*

Better was 11 ... ♗b7, but it was difficult to foresee all the consequences of the move played.

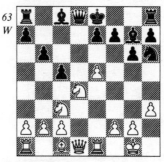

12 ♘c6!!

"The main feature of White's programme, announced with his tenth move. The knight voluntarily jumps into a trap." — Kholmov.

12 ... ♕d7

On 12 ... ♕xd1 13 ♖xd1 ♗b7 White had prepared a spectacular reply: 14 ♘b5! ♗xc6 15 ♘c7+ ♔f8 16 ♘xa8, and the knight cannot be taken because of the mate on d8.

13 ♘xe7!

The frisky knight sacrifices itself, eliminating the pawn which was the black king's main protection and at the same time enticing the king or the queen into an attack from the other knight. As a result, White gains a very important tempo for his offensive.

13 ... ♔xe7

In Kholmov's opinion the best defence was 13 ... ♕xe7 14 ♘d5 ♕d8 15 ♘f6+ ♗xf6 (15 ... ♔e7 16 ♗g5 ♕xd1 17 ♖axd1 ♗e6 18 ♘h5+! ♔f8 19 ♘xg7 ♔xg7 20 ♗f6+ ♔g8 21 g4!) 16 ef+ ♗e6 17 ♗xh6 ♕xf6, but here too the quiet 18 c3! would have secured White the advantage, since the black king cannot manage to hide safely: if 18 ... ♖d8 then 19 ♕a4+; if 18 ... g5 then 19 ♕d5!. However, 13 ... ♕xd1 would fail to 14 ♖xd1 ♔xe7 15 ♗g5+! ♔e6 16 ♖d6+ ♔f5 17 f4! (17 ... ♗e6 18 ♘e2!; 17 ... ♗xe5 18 ♖d5 f6 19 ♗xh6).

14 ♗xh6 ♗xh6 (64)

If 14 ... ♕xd1 then White plays 15 ♗g5+.

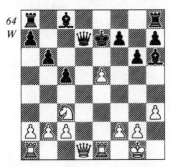

15 ♕f3! ♗g7

Black could not have saved the game by playing 15 ... ♖e8, as White had intended the following variation: 16 e6! fe 17 ♖ad1 ♕b7 18 ♘d5+ ♔d6 19 ♘b4+! ♔c7 20 ♕g3+ e5 21 ♖xe5!.

16 ♘d5+ ♔d8

Other retreats by the king also do not help: if 16 ... ♔e8 then 17 ♘f6+ ♗xf6 18 ef+ and 19 ♕xa8, and on 16 ... ♔f8 there follows 17 e6! ♕b7 18 e7+ ♔e8 19 ♕f6! ♕xd5 (19 ... ♗xf6 20 ♘xf6 mate) 20 ♕xg7 ♕d4 21 ♖e5!.

17 ♖ad1 ♗b7

An attempt to get the queen off the dangerous file with 17 ... ♕b7 would have been refuted by 18 e6! fe 19 ♘b4+!.

Now in the event of 19 ... ♔e8 or 19 ... ♔e7 White wins the queen by continuing 20 ♖xe6+! or 20 ♘c6+ respectively, and after 19 ... ♔c7 Black is mated: 20 ♕g3+ e5 21 ♖xe5 (threatening 22 ♖e7 mate) 21 ... cb 22 ♖c5 mate.

Also bad for Black is 19 ... ♗d4, in view of 20 ♖xd4+! cd 21 ♕f6+ ♔c7 22 ♕e5+ ♔d7 23 ♕xd4+ ♔c7 24 ♕e5+! ♔d7 25 ♖d1+ ♔e7 26 ♕g7+ ♔e8 27 ♕xh8+.

| | 18 | ♕b3 | ♗c6 | *(65)* |

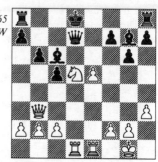

| | 19 | ♘xb6! |

The conclusive combination, based on exploiting the pin along the d-file.

19	...	ab
20	♕xf7!	♗xe5
21	♖xd7+	♗xd7
22	♖xe5	♔c7
23	♖e7	♖ad8
24	a4	g5
25	♕d5	♖he8
26	♖xh7	g4
27	a5	gh
28	ab+	♔xb6
29	♖xd7	Black resigned.

Game No. 23
Klinger–A. Kiss
Oberwart 1988

1	e4	c5
2	♘f3	♘c6
3	d4	cd

4	♘xd4	♘f6
5	♘c3	d6
6	f4	e5
7	♘f3	♗e7
8	♗c4	

An alternative way to develop the bishop is 8 ♗d3; there may follow: 8 ... ♛b6 9 ♖b1 0–0 10 ♛e2 ♗g4 11 ♗e3 ♛a5 12 h3 ♗xf3 13 ♛xf3 d5 14 ♗d2 ♘d4 15 ♛f2 de 16 ♘xe4 ♛xa2 with some advantage to Black (Cabrilo–Am. Rodriguez, Pancevo 1987).

8	...	♛b6?!

This attempt to seize the initiative immediately is risky; quieter is 8 ... 0–0.

9	♗b3	0–0
10	♛d3?! *(66)*	

A dubious move. It is hardly a good idea to place the queen on a square where it can be attacked. Better was 10 f5 h6 11 g4! and now after 11 ... ♘xg4 12 ♛e2 ♘d4 13 ♘xd4 ♗h4+ 14 ♔f1 ♛xd4 15 ♖g1 ♛f2+ 16 ♛xf2 ♘xf2 17 ♗xh6 White gets an advantage (Bronstein–Barczay, Szombathely 1966).

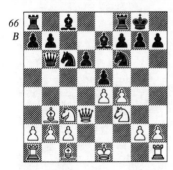

66
B

10	...	d5!?

An immediate reaction to the unnatural formation of the white pieces.

11	♘xd5	

On 11 fe, there follows 11 ... de 12 ♘xe4 ♘xe5! 13 ♘xe5 ♛a5+; Black also gets the initiative in the event of 11 ed e4! 12 ♘xe4 ♘b4 13 ♛e2 (dangerous for White is 13 ♘xf6+ ♗xf6 14 ♛e3 ♗f5!) 13 ... ♗g4! 14 ♘xf6+ ♗xf6 15 ♗e3 ♛a5 16 0–0 ♗xb2 17 ♖ab1 ♗c3.

11	...	♘xd5

12 ♗xd5?

A significant inaccuracy. The natural continuation 12 ed ♘b4
13 ♕e2 e4 14 ♘e5 would have allowed White to solve his problems.

| 12 | ... | ♘b4 |
| 13 | ♕b3 | ef! |

Thanks to this move Black opens the e-file.

14	♗xf4	♘xd5
15	ed	♗b4+!
16	♔d1	

No better was 16 ♗d2, because of 16 ... ♗xd2+ 17 ♘xd2
♖e8+ 18 ♔f1 ♕c5, followed by 19 ... ♗f5.

16	...	♗g4
17	♗e3	♕d6
18	♔c1	♖ac8
19	♖d1	♖c7

In his notes to this game Stohl gives this move a question-
mark, considering the strongest continuation to be 19 ... ♖fe8.
Nevertheless, also after the move in the game it is not easy for
White to find the correct defence.

| 20 | ♖d4 | ♗xf3 |
| 21 | gf | |

On 21 ♕xb4, there would have followed 21 ... ♕xh2!.

| 21 | ... | ♖fc8 *(67)* |

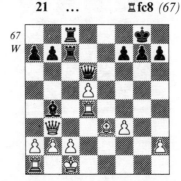

A critical position. The only playable continuation for White is
22 ♕xb4 ♖xc2+ 23 ♔d1, when after either 23 ... ♕xh2 24 ♕e1
♕g2 25 ♗d2! ♕xf3+ 26 ♕e2 ♕h1+ 27 ♕e1, or 23 ... ♕f6 24
♖f4! ♕a6 25 ♕e1 ♕d3+ 26 ♗d2, he maintains the equilibrium
(analysis by Stohl). Bad is 22 ♗f4 ♕c5 23 ♖xb4 ♕g1+ 24 ♔d2

♖xc2+ 25 ♕xc2 ♕f2+. As for the move in the game, it led to a spectacular finish.

22   ♖xb4?   ♖xc2+
23   ♔b1

It would be bad to continue 23 ♔d1 ♕xh2, or 23 ♕xc2 ♖xc2+ 24 ♔xc2 ♕xb4 25 ♖d1 ♕c4+ 26 ♔b1 ♕e2.

23   ...   ♕g6
24   ♖e4 *(68)*

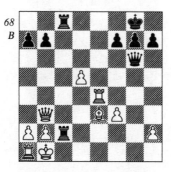

24   ...   ♕g1+!

The bishop is deflected from the c1-square: 25 ♗xg1 ♖c1 mate.
White resigned.

Game No. 24
De Firmian–Ehlvest
Reggio Emilia 1989/90

1	e4	c5
2	♘f3	e6
3	d4	cd
4	♘xd4	♘f6
5	♘c3	d6
6	f4	♗e7
7	♕f3	0–0
8	♗e3	e5
9	♘f5	♗xf5
10	ef	♕a5

An extremely useful move: the black queen pins the knight on c3 and takes control of the e5-square.

11   g4

Now Black cannot delay.

11	...	e4
12	♕d1	d5
13	g5?! *(69)*	

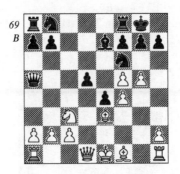

13	...	♘c6!
14	gf	♗xf6

Black's big lead in development and the weakness of the white f-pawns allow us to assess Black's compensation as more than adequate.

15	♕d2	♗h4+
16	♔d1	

White's position would be quite bad after 16 ♗f2 e3! 17 ♕xe3 ♖fe8.

16	...	d4
17	♘xe4	♕xf5
18	♘g3	♗xg3
19	hg	de
20	♗d3! *(70)*	

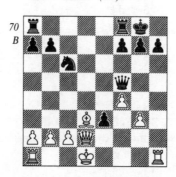

White has conducted a difficult defence quite well and, it would appear, is close to equality, but a pin on the d-file turns out to be fatal.

20   ...   **♖ad8!**

20 ... ed 21 ♗xf5 g6 22 ♗e4 leads to a position with clearly drawish tendencies.

21   **♕c3**

Better was 21 ♕xe3, although also in this case after 21 ... ♘b4 (but not 21 ... ♖fe8 22 ♕xe8+!) 22 ♔d2 ♘xd3 23 cd ♕a5+! 24 ♔d1 ♕d5 White's position is extremely difficult.

21   ...   **♕e4**

22   **♖g1** *(71)*

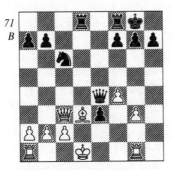

Now an elegant combination is decisive, based on motifs arising from the pin.

22	**...**	**♖xd3+!**
23	**cd**	**♖d8!**
24	**♔c2**	**♖xd3!**
25	**♕xd3**	**♘b4+**
26	**♔c3**	**♘xd3**

White resigned.

5 Tactical Success

Quite frequently spectacular combinations and interesting tactical operations are carried out in the absence of any resistance on the opponent's part. But when players of roughly equal standard do battle in the Sicilian, the game is full of ingenious ideas, subtle tactical plans and cunning traps.

In the games quoted below, one side emerges triumphant after a very sharp and complicated struggle, having overcome counterplay from his opponent.

Typical of such games is an exchange of tactical blows (real and apparent) with the aim of fighting for the initiative. We shall quote an example of successful counter-operations directed against active play from the opponent.

Hawelko–Afek
Berlin 1990

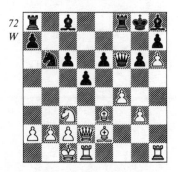

This position was reached after one of the rarer lines of the Dragon. The outcome of the game will depend to a considerable extent of the fight for control of the dark squares, a fight which involves various tactical subtleties.

19   ♗c5   ♖b8!

Black has no intention of losing a tempo by retreating his rook from f8, quite reasonably reckoning on getting excellent attacking opportunities in the event of the rook's capture by the white bishop.

20	♗d6	♗d7!
21	♗e5	♕e7
22	♗xh8	♔xh8
23	♕d4+	e5!

This move cuts across White's plans with great effect.

| 24 | fe |

A risky reply: sounder was 24 ♕xe5+ ♕xe5 25 fe ♖be8 26 ♖hf1 ♔g8 27 ♔d2.

24	...	c5!
25	♕h4	♕xe5
26	♖he1	g5!
27	♕h1	

It would be bad for White to play 27 ♕h2, in view of 27 ... ♕e3+ 28 ♔b1 ♖f2 29 ♕g1 ♘c4! 30 ♗xc4 ♕xc3 31 ♗b3 ♖xb3! with mate.

27	...	♕xg3
28	♗d3	♖f7
29	♘xd5	♗c6
30	♗e4	♘c4

The start of a decisive storm.

| 31 | b3 | ♕e5! |
| 32 | c3 | |

The knight cannot be taken: 32 bc ♖f2 33 c3 ♗xd5.

| 32 | ... | ♗xd5 |
| 33 | ♖d3 | ♕f4+ |

White resigned.

Game No. 25
Ambroz–Rausis
W. Germany 1989/90

1	e4	c5
2	♘f3	♘c6
3	♗b5	d6

Play has transposed to the Khachaturov Variation, which was worked out in 1937.

| 4 | 0–0 | ♗g4 |

A logical continuation, with which Black fights for control of the important central square d4.

5   h3

The immediate 5 c3 also does not give White any advantage; Black's strongest continuation is 5 ... ♘f6 6 ♖e1 e6 (6 ... ♕b6!?) 7 d3 ♘d7.

5	...	♗h5
6	c3	♕b6
7	♗a4	

In the game Kasparyan–Bronstein, 20th USSR Ch., 1952, there followed: 7 ♘a3 a6 8 ♗e2 e6! 9 d3 ♘f6 10 ♘h2 ♗g6 11 ♔h1 d5 with full equality.

7	...	♘f6
8	♖e1	

In this position there is an interesting pawn sacrifice: 8 d4!?; after 8 ... cd 9 cd ♗xf3 10 ♕xf3 ♕xd4 11 ♘c3 White has quite good prospects; play is unclear after 9 ... d5 10 e5 ♘e4 11 g4 ♗g6 12 e6 f6, or 10 ♘c3 0–0–0!.

8	...	e6
9	d4	cd
10	cd	d5
11	ed	♘xd5
12	♘c3	0–0–0?!

More cautious was 12 ... ♖d8.

13	♗xc6	♕xc6
14	♘xd5	♕xd5
15	g4	♗g6 *(73)*

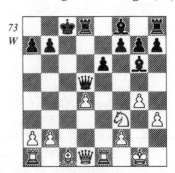

73
W

16   ♖e5?!

White would have had a strong attack after 16 ♗f4 ♗d6 17

♖c1+ ♔b8 18 ♖c5! ♕xa2 19 ♕d2, and now not 19 ... ♔a8
because of 20 ♗xd6 ♖xd6 21 ♕c3, with the threat of mate (22
♖c8+) or winning the queen (22 ♖a5).

	16	...	♕d7
	17	♗e3	♗d6
	18	♖a5	b6
	19	♘e5	♗xe5
	20	♖xe5	f6?! *(74)*

Now the game enters a period of unfathomable complications.
Quieter was 20 ... ♔b8 21 ♗f4 ♔a8.

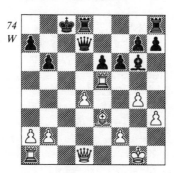

| | 21 | ♕f3! | fe |

On 21 ... ♔b8 White wins with 22 ♗f4.

	22	♕a8+	♔c7
	23	♕xa7+	♔d6
	24	♕a3+!	

Evidently Black had been counting on 24 ♕xb6+.

	24	...	♔c6
	25	♕a6	ed
	26	♖c1+	♔d5

It would be bad to play 26 ... ♔d6, because of 27 ♕xb6+ ♔e7
28 ♗g5+ ♔e8 29 ♖c7.

| | 27 | ♕c4+ | ♔e5 |
| | 28 | ♗g5 | |

The threat is 29 f4+ ♔e4 30 ♖e1+ with mate.

| | 28 | ... | ♖df8 *(75)* |
| | 29 | f4+? | |

Black could hardly have succeeded in saving the game after 29
♖e1+ ♔e4 30 ♕d3 ♕c6 (but not 30 ... ♕d5 because of 31 ♕g3
mate!) 31 f3.

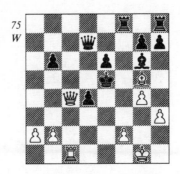

29	...	ⴄxf4
30	♗xf4+	♔xf4
31	♕e2	♔g5!

Now on 32 ⴄf1 there follows 32 ... ♗f5!.

32	♕e5+	♔h4
33	ⴄf1	♕d5
34	♕xg7?	(76)

White has lost his sense of danger. It was essential to take a draw by perpetual check: 34 ♕e1+ ♔g5 35 ♕d2+ ♔h4 36 ♕e1+. In the event of 34 ... ♔xh3 35 ⴄf2 it is Black who risks losing.

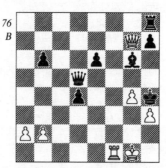

34	...	♔g3!

The black king goes onto the attack. The threat is 35 ... ♕g2 mate.

35	♕c7+	e5
36	ⴄf2	ⴄf8!

With the aim of diverting the white rook.

37	ⴄd2	♕h1+!

But now the white king is enticed into a mate: 38 ♔xh1 ♖f1 mate. White resigned.

Game No. 26
Plaskett–Watson
Brighton 1984

1	e4	c5
2	♘f3	d6
3	d4	cd
4	♘xd4	♘f6
5	♘c3	g6
6	♗e3	♗g7
7	f3	0–0
8	♕d2	♘c6
9	g4	♗e6!

A very strong move. Now in the event of 10 ♘xe6 fe 11 0–0–0 ♘e5 12 ♗e2 ♖c8 Black gets the advantage. For example: 13 ♘b5 ♕d7 14 ♘a3 b5 15 ♖hf1 ♘c4 16 ♘xc4 bc 17 c3 ♕a4 18 ♔b1 ♖c6 (Sveshnikov–van der Wiel, Sochi 1980).

10	0–0–0	♘xd4
11	♗xd4	♕a5
12	a3	♖fc8

Worth considering is 12 … ♖ab8 13 h4 b5 14 ♘d5 ♕xd2+ 15 ♖xd2 ♗xd5 16 ed b4.

13	h4	♖ab8
14	h5	

White gets some advantage after 14 ♘d5 ♕xd2+ 15 ♖xd2 ♘xd5 16 ♗xg7 ♘e3 17 ♗d4 ♘xf1 18 ♖xf1 b6 19 g5! (Short–Sax, Hastings 1983/84).

14	…	b5
15	h6 *(77)*	
15	…	b4!?

This is better than 15 … ♗h8?! 16 ♘d5 ♕xd2+ 17 ♖xd2 ♘xd5 18 ed ♗xd4 19 ♖xd4, with a small advantage to White (Tal–Sax, Moscow IZ 1982).

But Black had the paradoxical move 15 … ♗f8!!, when there could have followed: 16 ♗xf6 b4!! 17 ♗d4 ba 18 b3 ♗xb3! 19 cb ♖xb3 20 ♗d3 a2! 21 ♔c2 ♕a4 22 ♗c4 ♖xc4 (analysis by Schneider and Sapi in *Sicilian Dragon: Classical and Levenfish Variations*).

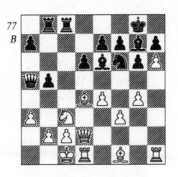

16	hg	ba
17	♕h6	ab+
18	♔d2	*(78)*

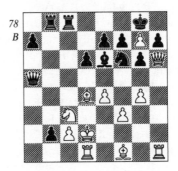

| 18 | ... | ♗xg4! |

The bishop comes into play with great effect. Now not 19 fg because of 19 ... e5! 20 ♔d3 ed 21 ♘d5 ♕b5+ 22 ♔d2 ♖xc2+! 23 ♔xc2 b1(♕)+ 24 ♖xb1 ♕xb1+.

| 19 | ♗xf6 | ♗h5 |
| 20 | ♗d4?! | |

White also gets a difficult game in other variations: 20 ♗h3 ef 21 ♗xc8 ♖xc8 22 ♕e3 ♕b4! when, despite having an extra rook, White is powerless against the advance of the a-pawn — for example, 23 ♖h4 d5! 24 ed ♕xh4 25 d6 ♕h2+ 26 ♔e1 ♕xc2; or 20 ♔e3 ♖xc3+ 21 ♗xc3 ♕xc3+ 22 ♗d3 a5!, and the black pawns cannot be held back; but nevertheless there was a saving move: 20 ♖xh5! gh 21 ♗h3 (but not 21 ♗d4 e5! when play transposes to what occurred in the game) 21 ... ef 22 ♗xc8 ♖xc8 23 ♕xf6 ♕b4 24 ♖b1 a5 25 ♔d3 ♕c4+ 26 ♔d2 ♕b4 27 ♔d3

♕c4+ 28 ♔d2 with a draw (Kondou–Jagodzinska, Katowice 1984).

20	...	e5
21	♖xh5	

White loses after 21 ♔d3 ed 22 ♘d5 ♖c3+ 23 ♔e2 ♖xc2+ 24 ♔d3 ♕b5+ 25 ♔xc2 b1(♕)+ 26 ♖xb1 ♕xb1+ 27 ♔d2 ♖b2 mate.

21	...	gh
22	♕g5	♕b4

Also sufficient was 22 ... b1(♕) 23 ♖xb1 ♖xb1 24 ♗h3 ♖c4! 25 ♔e2 ♖xd4 26 ♗f5 ♕a6+, or 24 ♗d3 ♖a1.

23	♗d3	♕xd4
24	♘d5	♕f2+
25	♗e2	♖xc2+
26	♔xc2	♕xe2+
27	♔c3	♕xf3+
28	♔c4	♕b3 mate.

Game No. 27
Ivanchuk–A. Schneider
Debrecen 1988

1	e4	c5
2	♘f3	d6
3	d4	cd
4	♘xd4	♘f6
5	♘c3	g6
6	♗e3	♗g7
7	f3	0–0
8	♕d2	♘c6
9	♗c4	♗d7
10	h4	♘e5
11	♗b3	♖c8
12	0–0–0	♘c4
13	♗xc4	♖xc4
14	g4	

In recent years a more common continuation has been 14 h5.

14	...	♕c7

This move has a good reputation, as does 14 ... b5, see Game 55; Kokkonen–Nesis.

15	h5	♖c8
16	hg	fg

17 &b1 b5 (79)

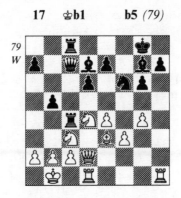

A critical position: after the tempting 18 ♕h2 Black had prepared an exchange sacrifice: 18 ... ♖xc3 19 bc ♕xc3 with an excellent game.

18 ♘d5! ♘xd5
19 ed a5?

Too careless. Better was 19 ... ♕b7 or 19 ... ♗e5! (taking away the h2-square from the white queen) 20 ♕f2 ♖f8! 21 ♕h4 ♖f7.

20 ♕h2 h6
21 b3!

It turns out that on 21 ... ♖c3? there would follow 22 ♗xh6 ♗xd4 23 ♖xd4 ♖xc2 24 ♗d2!.

21 ... ♖b4
22 ♖d3!

A more complicated game would have arisen after 22 a3 ♕c3 23 ab! (but not 23 ♖d3 ♖xb3+!) 23 ... ♕xe3 24 ♖d3 ♕g5 25 ba.

22 ... a4
23 ♕d2 ♖c4!? (80)

Black would have had no counter-chances at all after 23 ... ab 24 ♕xb4 ♗xd4 25 ♕xb3. As far as the rook sacrifice is concerned, it is correct: 24 bc bc 25 ♖c3 ♖b8+ 26 &a1 (or 26 &c1 ♕b7 27 &d1 ♕xd5) 26 ... ♕b6 27 ♕c1 ♗xd4, and Black has sufficient compensation for the exchange.

24 ♗xh6! ♗xd4
25 bc!

Precisely so, and not 25 ♖xd4 ♖xd4 26 ♕xd4 ♕xc2+ 27 &a1 ♕c3+.

25 ... ♗e5
26 ♗f4 ♗g7

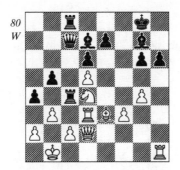

After the natural 26 ... bc White had prepared 27 ♗xe5 cd 28 ♕h6!!.

	27	c5!

A subtle move: White does not allow the b-file to be opened.

27	...	♕xc5
28	♗e3	♕c4
29	♗d4	e5
30	de	♗xe6
31	♗xg7	♕xa2+
32	♔c1	♔xg7
33	♕h6+	♔f7
34	♕h7+	

But not 34 ♕f4+?? ♔g8, when White is in trouble.

34	...	♔f6
35	g5+	♔f5 (81)

Black cannot take the pawn on g5 with his king, because of 36 ♖g1+ ♔f4 37 ♕h6+ ♔e5 38 ♕g5+ with mate.

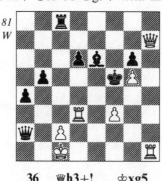

36	♕h3+!	♔xg5
37	♕h4+	♔f5

| 38 | ♕g4+ | ♔f6 |
| 39 | ♕f4+ | |

A very interesting attack: first White lured the black king into the centre, and now he has begun to drive it back to the edge of the board.

| 39 | ... | ♔e7 |

No better was 39 ... ♔g7 40 ♕d4+.

40	♖h7+	♔e8
41	♖h8+	♗g8
42	♖e3+	♔d7 *(82)*

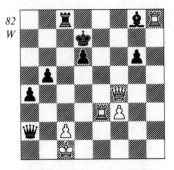

82
W

| 43 | ♕g4+ | ♔d8 |

Playing 43 ... ♔c7 would not help, because of 44 ♖c3+. If 43 ... ♗e6 then 44 ♕xe6+! ♕xe6 45 ♖h7+ is decisive.

| 44 | ♖e8+! | |

After 44 ... ♔xe8 45 ♕xc8+ ♔e7 46 ♕xg8 ♕a1+ the white king escapes from perpetual check: 47 ♔d2 ♕d4+ 48 ♔e2 ♕e5+ 49 ♔f1 ♕a1+ 50 ♔g2.

Black resigned.

Game No. 28
Anand–Benjamin
Wijk aan Zee 1989

1	e4	c5
2	♘f3	d6
3	d4	cd
4	♘xd4	♘f6
5	♘c3	♘c6
6	♗g5	e6
7	♕d2	♗e7

8	0–0–0	0–0
9	♘b3	♛b6

9 … a6 is considered in Game 53; Yudasin–Aseev.

10	f3	♖d8
11	♔b1	d5?!

This thrust is more effective after a preliminary 11 … a6 12 h4, when White's pawn structure on the kingside has been weakened.

12	♗xf6!	de? *(83)*

Black has clearly over-estimated his possibilities. He should have preferred the natural 12 … ♗xf6, although after 13 ed ♗xc3 14 ♛xc3 ed 15 ♛c5 White has some advantage.

13	♗xe7!	♖xd2
14	♘xd2	

This move is the essence of the tactical refutation of Black's unjustified activity. Now Black would lose after 14 … ♘xe7, because of 15 ♘c4 ♛c7 16 ♘b5.

14	…	ef
15	gf?!	

White misses his chance to derive maximum benefit from the position which has now arisen. After 15 ♘c4! ♛c7 (quite bad is 15 … ♛f2, because of 16 ♘e4) 16 ♗d6 fg 17 ♗xg2 ♛d8 18 ♗g3 ♛e7 19 ♖he1 Black cannot avoid a decisive invasion by the white pieces.

15	…	e5
16	♗h4	

16 ♗a3 looks preferable.

16	…	♗e6
17	♘de4	

17 ♗c4 ♗xc4 18 ♘xc4 would be bad, because of 18 … ♛b4!.

17	...	♘d4
18	♗g2	

More accurate was 18 ♗f2 at once.

18	...	♖c8
19	♗f2	f5! *(84)*

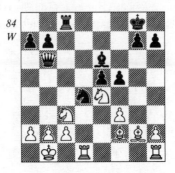

| 20 | f4! | |

In Black's favour is 20 ♘g5? ♖xc3! 21 ♘xe6 ♕xe6 22 ♗xd4 (quite bad for White is 22 bc ♕b6+ 23 ♔c1 ♘e2+ 24 ♔d2 ♕xf2) 22 ... ed 23 bc dc 24 ♔a1 ♕e2! 25 ♖hg1 ♕xc2 26 ♖b1 ♕d2.

20	...	fe
21	fe	♖c4

Worth considering was 21 ... ♖d8!, and now after the natural 22 ♖he1 (22 ♘e2? is bad because of 22 ... ♗xa2+) Black equalises with 22 ... ♗g4! 23 ♖d2 ♕h6! 24 ♗e3 (not 24 ♖xd4, in view of 24 ... ♖xd4 25 ♗xd4 ♕d2) 24 ... ♕h4.

The only chance for White to maintain his advantage would have been offered by the continuation 22 ♖d2! ♗f5 23 ♗e3!.

| 22 | ♖he1 | |

Strong was the — at first sight — extremely risky move 22 ♘e2!. Now a tempting queen sacrifice — 22 ... ♕xb2+ 23 ♔xb2 ♖xc2+ 24 ♔a1 ♘xe2 — would not be playable, because of the simple 25 ♗e1. Black also gets nowhere after 22 ... ♖a4 23 b3! ♖xa2 24 ♗xd4.

22	...	♖b4!?
23	♔c1	

As Joel Benjamin observes, it was possible to play 23 b3, in order on 23 ... ♗xb3 24 ab ♖xb3+ simply to move away with the king by playing 25 ♔c1.

23	...	♗g4?

Worth considering was the continuation 23 ... ♖xb2 (Black loses after 23 ... ♘b3+ 24 ab ♕xf2 25 ♖d8+ ♔f7 26 ♖f1) 24 ♗xd4 ♕b4.

24	♘d5	♕c5
25	♘xb4	♗xd1
26	♔xd1!	

But not 26 ♖xd1? ♘e2+.

26	...	e3
27	♖xe3	♘f5 *(85)*

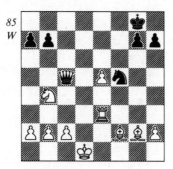

85
W

28	♗d5+!	

White cannot play 28 ♖f3 ♕xb4 29 ♖xf5, because of 29 ... ♕g4+.

28	...	♔f8
29	♖f3	♕xb4
30	♖xf5+	♔e8
31	e6	Black resigned.

Game No. 29
Malinin–Kribun
corr. 1988/89

1	e4	c5
2	♘f3	♘c6
3	d4	cd
4	♘xd4	♘f6
5	♘c3	d6
6	♗c4	

The point of this move, with which the Sozin Attack begins, is that it prepares for a pawn storm on the kingside with f2–f4–f5 and, in some lines, g2–g4. This move also renders harmless the counter-thrust ... e7–e5, after which White would play ♘d4–e2 with an active position.

6	...	♕b6
7	♘b3	e6
8	♕e2	

There are other continuations deserving consideration: 8 ♗g5, when it is possible to continue 8 ... a6 9 0–0 ♘e5 10 ♗e2 ♗e7 11 ♔h1 0–0 12 f4 ♘g6 13 ♗d3 h6 14 f5 ♘e5 15 ♗h4 ♗d7 16 fe fe 17 ♕e2 ♖f7 with approximate equality (A. Sokolov–Tukmakov, USSR Ch., Odessa 1989); or 8 0–0 a6 9 a4 ♕c7 10 a5 ♗e7 11 ♗e2 ♘d7! 12 ♗f4 0–0 13 ♕d3 ♘de5 14 ♕g3 ♗d7 15 ♖fd1 ♘b4 16 ♗h6 ♘g6 17 ♗g5 ♗xg5 18 ♕xg5 ♖fd8 19 ♕d2 ♗e8, also with equality (van der Wiel–Timman, Rotterdam 1989). The move in the game does not promise White an opening advantage, but it leads to very sharp play.

8	...	♗e7
9	f4	0–0
10	♗e3	♕c7
11	0–0–0	a6
12	g4!?	b5
13	♗d3	♘b4
14	g5	♘d7
15	♖hg1	♘xd3+!

In the event of 15 ... ♗b7 it looks very strong for White to play 16 e5!, when he gets a lasting initiative: 16 ... ♘xd3+ (if 16 ... de then 17 ♗xh7+ ♔xh7 18 ♕h5+ ♔g8 19 ♖g3 ♗e4 20 ♖h3 f6 21 g6 ♗xg6 22 ♕xg6 ♖fc8 23 ♖g1 ♗f8 24 ♖h7 ♘b8 25 ♕h5 with mate) 17 ♕xd3 d5 18 h4 ♕c4 19 ♕xc4 bc 20 ♘d4 ♗b4 21 ♘ce2 ♘c5 22 a3 ♗a5 23 h5.

16	♖xd3	b4 *(86)*
17	♗d4!!?	

A totally unexpected move. Black was counting on seizing the initiative after 17 ♘d1 (17 ♘b1) 17 ... a5 18 ♕h5 ♗a6 19 ♖d2 a4.

17	...	bc
18	♕h5!	

All other continuations are much less sharp. In the event of 18 ♖h3 g6! 19 ♖g4 e5 20 ♖gh4 ♘c5, or 19 ♖xh7 ♔xh7 20 ♕g4 e5 21 ♕h4+ ♔g8 22 ♖g3 f6, White's attack is stifled. On 18 ♖xc3,

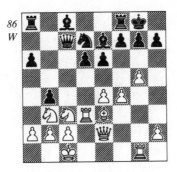

there follows 18 ... ♕b7 19 ♖h3 g6! 20 ♘a5 ♕b5 21 ♕e1 e5 22 c4 ♕a4 23 ♖a3 ♕xa3! 24 ba ed 25 ♘c6 ♖e8 and Black gets the advantage.

	18	...	cb+
	19	♔b1	

It would not be good to play 19 ♔xb2, since in the variation 19 ... ♖d8 20 ♗xg7 ♔xg7 21 ♕h6+ ♔h8 22 g6 fg 23 ♖xg6 Black has the possibility of 23 ... ♗f6+! 24 ♖xf6 ♘xf6 25 ♕xf6+ ♕g7.

| | 19 | ... | ♖d8?!! |

Worth considering was 19 ... ♗b7!. Now on 20 ♖c3 a very strong move is 20 ... ♕d8!, when the following line is possible: 21 ♘d2! (White gets nowhere with 21 ♗xg7 ♗xe4 22 ♕h6 ♖e8!) 21 ... ♖e8 22 ♖h3 ♘f8 23 g6! fg 24 ♖xg6! e5! 25 fe de! 26 ♖xg7+ ♔xg7 27 ♕h6+ ♔f7 28 ♕h5+ ♔g8 29 ♖g3+ ♗g5!! 30 ♖xg5+ ♔h8! (but not 30 ... ♘g6 31 ♖xg6+ hg 32 ♕xg6+ ♔f8 33 ♕f5+ with perpetual check) 31 ♕h6 ♕xg5 32 ♕xg5 ed and Black has the advantage.

	20	♗xg7!	♔xg7
	21	♕h6+	♔h8

It would be bad to play 21 ... ♔g8, because of 22 g6 hg 23 ♖xg6+ hg 24 ♕xg6 ♔f8 25 ♖h3 ♗f6 26 ♖h7.

	22	g6	fg
	23	♖xg6	♖g8!

On 23 ... ♗f6 there follows 24 ♖g4 with the irresistible threat of 25 ♕xh7+; and after 23 ... ♗f8 decisive is 24 ♕h4 ♗g7 25 ♖xg7 ♔xg7 26 ♖g3+ ♔h8 27 ♕g5.

	24	♖xg8+	♔xg8
	25	♖g3+	♔f7 *(87)*

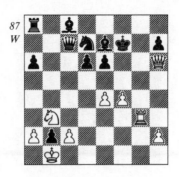

26   &g7+?

A tempting continuation, but not the best. White should have brought his last reserves into battle: 26 &d4! and now after 26 ... &f6 27 e5 de 28 fe ♕c4! (but not 28 ... ♕xe5? because of 29 &g7+ &e8 30 &xe7 &xe7 31 &c6+ &d6 32 &xe5 &xe5 33 ♕g5+ and 34 ♕xf6) 29 &g7+ &e8 30 &xe7+ &xe7 31 ♕g7+! &d8 32 ef a position arises in which White is a rook down, but nevertheless the most likely outcome is a draw. For example: 32 ... &d7 33 ♕f8+ &c7 34 ♕xa8 ♕xd4 35 ♕f8 ♕d6 36 ♕g7 ♕d1+ 37 &xb2 ♕d4+ 38 &b1 &c6 39 ♕g2+ &d6 40 ♕g7, or 32 ... ♕f1+ 33 &xb2 &b8+ 34 &b3 &d7 (worse is 34 ... &b7? 35 ♕f8+ &d7 36 f7 ♕f6+ 37 c3 ♕e7 38 ♕g8) 35 f7 &c7 36 ♕e5+ &c8 37 ♕h8+ &c7 (37 ... &b7 leads to a spectacular finish: 38 &c5+ &a8+ 39 ♕xb8+!! &xb8 40 f8(♕)+ ♕xf8 41 &d7+ and 42 &xf8) 38 ♕e5+ &c8.

26   ...   &e8
27   ♕xe6   &f6!

Unsuccessful would be 27 ... &f8 28 ♕f7+ &d8 29 f5 &a7 30 &g8 (but not 30 f6? &e6!) 30 ... ♕c3 31 f6 ♕xf6 32 &xf8+ &c7 33 ♕c4+.

28   ♕f7+   &d8
29   &d4   &a7
30   e5 *(88)*
30   ...   de!

Despite having two (!) extra pieces Black needs a certain degree of accuracy. For example, the passive 30 ... &e8 would have led to a difficult position for Black after 31 &g8 ♕d7 32 f5 ♕a4 33 f6 &xf6 34 ♕xf6 &c7 35 ♕e7+ &b6 36 ♕d8+.

31   fe   ♕c3!

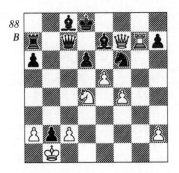

88
B

32	ef	♕e1+
33	♔xb2	♗a3+
34	♔xa3	♕c1+
35	♔b4	♖xf7
36	♖xf7	♕f4
37	♖f8+	♔c7
38	♔c3	♕e3+

White resigned.

Game No. 30
Fischer–Geller
Skopje 1967

1	e4	c5
2	♘f3	d6
3	d4	cd
4	♘xd4	♘f6
5	♘c3	♘c6
6	♗c4	e6

Worth considering is Benko's move 6 ... ♕b6!?. In the game Fischer–Saidy, USA Ch. 1966/67, a double-edged position arose after 7 ♘b3 e6 8 0–0 ♗e7 9 ♗e3 ♕c7 10 f4 0–0 11 ♗d3. See also Game 29; Malinin–Kribun, where White tried 8 ♕e2.

7 ♗e3

Another possibility is 7 ♗b3. The game Fischer–Dely, Skopje 1967, continued: 7 ... a6 8 f4! ♕a5 9 0–0 ♘xd4? 10 ♕xd4 d5 11 ♗e3 ♘xe4 12 ♘xe4 de 13 f5! ♕b4 14 fe ♗xe6 15 ♗xe6! fe 16 ♖xf8+! ♕xf8 17 ♕a4+ and Black resigned.

7 ... ♗e7

Fischer considered that Black should have begun operations on the queenside speedily with 7 ... a6 8 ♗b3 ♕c7 9 ♕e2 b5 10 0-0-0 ♘a5 (or 10 ... ♗b7).

8 ♗b3 0-0
9 ♕e2

Preparing to castle queenside and not allowing the move ... ♘f6-g4, which would have followed in reply to 9 ♕d2.

9 ... ♕a5

Geller attempts to strengthen this variation and rejects the usual 9 ... a6. The game Velimirovic–Nikolic, Belgrade 1964, continued: 9 ... a6 10 0-0-0 ♕c7 11 g4 ♘xd4 12 ♖xd4! b5 (on 12 ... e5 interesting is an exchange sacrifice suggested by Tal: 13 ♖c4! ♕d8 14 g5 ♘e8 15 ♖xc8! ♖xc8 16 h4 ♘c7 17 ♕g4 and then h4-h5 with a very strong attack) 13 g5 ♘d7 14 ♕h5 (14 ♖g1 was played in Game 7; Szmetan–G. Garcia) 14 ... ♘e5 15 f4 ♘c6 16 ♖d3 ♘b4 17 ♖d2 ♖d8 18 f5 g6 19 fg hg 20 ♕h4 ♘c6 21 ♕g3 ♘e5 22 h4 ♗b7 23 h5 b4 24 hg ♘xg6 25 ♖dh2 bc 26 ♗d4 e5 27 ♖h8+!! (destroying Black's fortifications) 27 ... ♘xh8 28 g6! ♗f6 29 gf++ ♔f8 30 ♖h7! and White won.

10 0-0-0 ♘xd4

Apparently Geller rejected 10 ... ♗d7, writes Fischer, because of 11 ♘db5! ♘e8 12 ♗f4 a6 13 ♘xd6 ♘xd6 14 ♗xd6 ♗xd6 15 ♖xd6 ♕g5+ 16 ♕d2 ♕xg2 17 ♖d1 ♗e8 18 ♕f4 with good pressure.

11 ♗xd4 ♗d7

Black cannot win a pawn with 11 ... ♕g5+ 12 ♔b1 ♕xg2?, in view of 13 ♖hg1 ♕h3 14 e5 ♘e8 15 ed ♗xd6 16 ♗xg7! ♘xg7 17 ♖xd6.

12 ♔b1 *(89)*

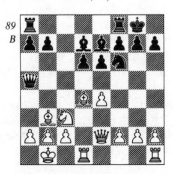

The first critical position. White's immediate threat is 13 ♗xf6.

| **12** | **...** | **♗c6** |

In the game Fischer–Sofrevski, from a subsequent round of the same tournament, Black tried to play more forcefully with 12 ... ♖ad8, but he lost after 13 ♕e3! b6 14 ♗xf6! gf (Black should have reconciled himself to the loss of a pawn: 14 ... ♗xf6 15 ♖xd6 ♗c8) 15 ♘d5!! ♖fe8 (if 15 ... ed then 16 ♖xd5 ♕a6 17 ♖h5! ♗g4 18 ♕g3) 16 ♘xe7+ (a quicker way to end the game was 16 ♕h6!) 16 ... ♖xe7 17 ♖xd6 ♖c8 18 ♕d4 ♗e8? 19 ♕xf6.

| **13** | **f4** | **♖ad8** |
| **14** | **♖hf1** | |

Also not bad was 14 f5 ef 15 ef ♖fe8 16 ♕f2, with a positional advantage.

| **14** | **...** | **b5** |
| **15** | **f5!** | |

Fischer does not waste time on the quiet 15 a3.

15	**...**	**b4**
16	**fe!**	**bc**
17	**ef+**	**♔h8**

Not 17 ... ♖xf7, because of 18 ♗xf7+ ♔xf7 19 ♕c4+ d5 20 ♕xc6.

| **18** | **♖f5** | **♕b4** |
| **19** | **♕f1!** | |

"A hard move to find — it took around 45 minutes," writes Fischer. The threat is 20 ♖xf6.

| **19** | **...** | **♘xe4** *(90)* |

Black would have lost immediately after 19 ... ♘d7 20 ♖h5 ♘e5 21 ♕f5 h6 22 ♕g6! and now if 22 ... ♘xg6 then 23 ♖xh6 mate. Fischer considers that 19 ... ♘g4 was objectively best, but after 20 ♗xc3 ♕b7 (20 ... ♕xe4 21 ♖d4!) 21 ♕f4 White would have had three pawns for a piece and a very strong attack.

| **20** | **a3?** | |

The winning move was 20 ♕f4, with the threat 21 ♖h5. Black has no satisfactory defence: 20 ... d5 21 ♕e5 ♘f6 22 ♖xf6 ♗xf6 23 ♕xf6!; 20 ... ♘d2+ 21 ♖xd2 cd 22 c3!! ♕xb3 23 ♗xg7+! ♔xg7 24 ♕g4+ ♔h8 25 ♕d4+; 20 ... cb 21 ♖h5! (threatening 22 ♗xg7+) 21 ... ♘c3+ (if 21 ... ♗f6 then 22 ♕f5 h6 23 ♖xh6+ gh 24 ♕g6! with inevitable mate) 22 ♔xb2 ♘xd1+ (or 22 ... ♖xf7 23 ♕xf7 ♘xd1+ 24 ♔b1! ♕xd4 25 ♖xh7+! ♔xh7 26 ♕h5 mate) 23 ♔c1 ♖xf7 24 ♗xf7! (24 ♕xf7? ♗g5+) when there is no defence against the threat of 25 ♖xh7+ ♔xh7 26 ♕f5+.

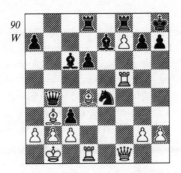

20	...	♕b7
21	♕f4	♗a4!!

Fischer had not foreseen this manoeuvre.

| 22 | ♕g4 |

22 ♕h6 ♗f6 23 ♖xf6 ♗xb3 also gives White nothing.

22	...	♗f6!
23	♖xf6	♗xb3! *(91)*

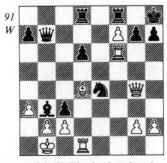

It turns out that on 24 cb Black simply plays 24 ... ♘xf6!, and if 24 ♖f4 then the discovered attack is decisive: 24 ... ♗a2+. White resigned.

Fischer called this game "a flawed masterpiece".

Game No. 31
Ehlvest–Smirin
USSR Ch., Moscow 1988

1	e4	c5
2	♘f3	d6
3	d4	cd
4	♘xd4	♘f6

5	♘c3	♘c6
6	♗c4	e6
7	♗e3	a6

In the game Yudasin–Rashkovsky, Kuibyshev 1986, there followed: 7 ... ♘a5 8 ♗d3 a6 9 f4, and after 9 ... b5 the advance 10 e5! gave White a considerable advantage: 10 ... de 11 fe ♘d5 12 ♕f3 ♘xe3 13 ♕xa8 ♗e7 14 ♘c6 ♘xc6 15 ♕xc6+ ♗d7 16 ♕e4.

8	♗b3	♘a5
9	f4	b5
10	e5	de
11	fe	♘xb3
12	ab	♘d5
13	♕f3 *(92)*	

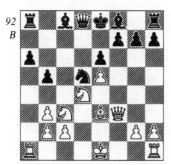

92
B

13	...	♘xe3?!

A tempting sacrifice, but Black had not calculated it right through to a conclusion. Worth considering was 13 ... ♗b7.

14	♕xa8	♕d7 *(93)*

93
W

15	♘cxb5	

This is the point! On 15 ... ab there follows 16 ♖a7.

	15	...	♘xg2+
	16	♕xg2	♗b7
	17	♕f1	ab

It turns out that Black loses after 17 ... ♗xh1 18 ♕xh1 ab 19 ♕a8+ ♕d8 20 ♕c6+ ♕d7 21 ♖a8+ ♔e7 22 ♕c5+.

	18	0-0-0	♗d5
	19	♘xb5	♕b7
	20	♖g1	g6
	21	♖d2!	*(94)*

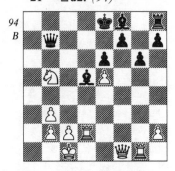

This move serves to underline White's total supremacy and makes it possible for him to proceed to a stage where he can turn his advantage into victory by a matter of technique.

	21	...	♗e7
	22	♘d6+	♗xd6
	23	ed	0-0
	24	♖g4	♕c6
	25	♕f6	♕xd6
	26	c4	♕c7
	27	♖gd4	♕c5
	28	b4!	

Depriving Black of the slightest counter-chance.

	28	...	♕c7
	29	b3	♖a8
	30	♖4d3!	

On 30 ... ♗xc4 there follows 31 ♖d8+.
Black resigned.

6 A Fighting Draw – Tactics Leading to Dynamic Equilibrium

In the games in this chapter, one side manages to find, as it were, 'a chink in the armour' – an exchange of tactical punches and counter-punches leads to a position of dynamic equilibrium. The final positions in such games have a drawish nature, by virtue of repetition of moves, perpetual check, or the fact that very few pieces remain on the board. A classical example is the famous game Alekhine–Botvinnik, in which White started a pawn storm against the enemy king straight from the opening and Black responded with energetic counterplay.

Alekhine–Botvinnik
Nottingham 1936

After the initial moves — 1 e4 c5 2 ♘f3 ♘c6 3 d4 cd 4 ♘xd4 ♘f6 5 ♘c3 d6 6 ♗e2 g6 7 ♗e3 ♗g7 8 ♘b3 0–0 9 f4 ♗e6 10 g4!? *(93)* — a position arose in which decisive action is required from Black.

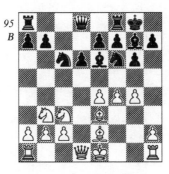

95
B

| 10 | ... | d5! |

This energetic counter in the centre leads to sharp, forcing play.

11	f5	

It would be bad to play 11 e5, because of 11 ... d4! 12 ♘xd4 ♘xd4 13 ♗xd4 ♘xg4.

11	...	♗c8
12	ed	♘b4
13	d6!	♕xd6
14	♗c5	♕f4
15	♖f1	

It would appear that White's plan has proved totally successful, but the tactical resources of Black's position are far from exhausted.

15	...	♕xh2
16	♗xb4	♘xg4!

This is the point: the bishop is deflected from the defence of the king.

17	♗xg4	♕g3+

Drawn by perpetual check.

Game No. 32
Grefe–Tarjan
USA Ch. 1973

1	e4	c5
2	♘f3	d6
3	d4	cd
4	♘xd4	♘f6
5	♘c3	g6
6	♗e3	♗g7
7	f3	♘c6
8	♕d2	0–0
9	♗c4	♗d7
10	h4	♖c8
11	♗b3	♘e5
12	h5	

This continuation was once considered the most forceful, but nowadays the most common choice is 12 0–0–0 (see Game 48; Kasparov–J. Piket). In the event of 12 ♗h6 ♗xh6 13 ♕xh6 ♖xc3! 14 bc ♕a5 15 ♕d2 ♖c8 Black gets counterplay in return for the exchange.

12	...	♘xh5
13	g4 *(96)*	

Again, after 13 ♗h6 ♗xh6 14 ♕xh6 Black would sacrifice the exchange on c3.

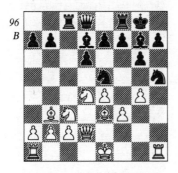

96
B

13 ... ♖c4!?

An interesting counter-punch, the idea of which is based on the fact that, in the event of 14 ♗xc4 ♘xc4 15 ♕e2 ♘xe3 16 ♕xe3 ♘f6, as compensation for the exchange Black gets the two bishops and a strong initiative.

14 gh ♖xd4
15 ♕g2

This would appear to be a logical continuation, particularly since after 15 ♕f2 an unpleasant reply is 15 ... ♖d3!, but White has the stronger 15 ♕e2!, when the bishop on e3 is defended.

15 ... ♕b6
16 hg

Black gets an excellent game after either 16 ♕f2 ♖c8 17 0-0 ♘c4 18 ♗xc4 ♖cxc4 19 ♘d5 ♕d8 20 b3 ♖xd5, or 16 0-0 ♘c4 17 ♗f2 (17 ♗xc4 ♕b2) 17 ... ♘d2 18 ♘e2 ♘xf1 19 ♖xf1 ♗b5 20 c4 ♗d7.

16 ... ♖xe4!
17 gf+ ♔h8 *(97)*
18 0-0-0

The rook sacrifice 18 ♖xh7+ would be simply refuted by 18 ... ♔xh7 19 ♕h2+ ♔g6 20 ♕g3+ ♘g4!. The move 18 fe, however, which was played in the game Eppinger–Berkell, Strasbourg 1973, led to White's defeat: 18 ... ♕xe3+ 19 ♕e2 ♕g3+ 20 ♕f2 ♘f3+ 21 ♔e2 ♘d4+ 22 ♔e1 ♘xc2+ 23 ♗xc2 ♗xc3+ 24 bc ♕xc3+.

18 ... ♕xe3+
19 ♔b1 ♖c4!

Blocking the bishop on b3.

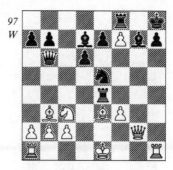

20	♖dg1	♖xf7
21	♗xc4	♘xc4
22	♕g6	*(98)*

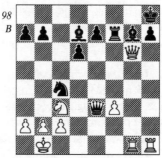

It seems that White is winning, but ...

22	...	♘a3+!
23	ba	

White would also get nowhere after 23 ♔a1 ♘xc2+ 24 ♕xc2 ♗f5 25 ♕b3 ♗e6.

23	...	♕b6+
24	♔c1	♕e3+
25	♔b1	Drawn.

Game No. 33

Kosenkov–Nesis

11th World Corr. Ch. Final 1983/85

1	e4	c5
2	♘f3	d6
3	d4	cd
4	♘xd4	♘f6

5	♘c3	g6
6	♗e3	♗g7
7	f3	0-0
8	♕d2	♘c6
9	0-0-0	d5
10	ed	

It used to be thought that 10 ♘xc6 bc amounts to simple transposition after 11 ed. But in the last few years there have been attempts in this variation to steer the game along a different path — 10 ♘xc6 bc 11 ♗h6 — with the aim of exchanging dark-squared bishops. This plan has not brought White any great success in practice, but Black needs to play energetically. For example:

(a) 11 ... ♕c7!? 12 ♗xg7 ♔xg7 13 ed (dubious is 13 ♕g5?! de 14 fe ♗e6 15 ♗e2 ♖ab8 16 ♕c5 a5 17 g3 ♕b7 with advantage to Black: V. Kostic–Kudrin, Valjevo 1984; but 13 h4 is worth considering) 13 ... cd 14 g4 (sharper is 14 h4 h5 15 ♘xd5 ♘xd5 16 ♕xd5 ♗e6 17 ♕d4+ ♔g8 18 ♗d3 ♖fd8 19 ♕e3 ♗xa2 20 g4 ♖ab8 with chances for both sides: A. Sokolov–Kudrin, Lugano 1985; in this variation it is dangerous for Black to allow White's h-pawn to advance by continuing, for example, 14 ... ♗e6?!, in view of 15 h5!, when it is bad to play 15 ... ♘xh5? 16 g4 ♘f6 17 ♕h6+ ♔g8 18 g5 ♘h5 19 ♖xh5 gh 20 ♗d3 f5 21 g6 and White wins; or 14 ... ♗b7?! 15 ♘b5! ♕c5? 16 h5 e5 17 ♕g5! ♕e7 18 hg fg 19 ♗d3 ♖fe8 20 ♗xg6! with a decisive attack: Renet–A. Romero, Barcelona 1985) 14 ... ♗b7 15 ♗d3?! (more precise is 15 ♕d4) 15 ... d4 16 ♘e4 ♘d5 and Black's position is already preferable (Veröci–Petronic – Chiburdanidze, Smederevska Palanka 1983).

(b) 11 ... ♕a5 12 ♗xg7 ♔xg7 13 e5 ♘g8 14 h4 ♗e6 15 h5 ♖ab8 with the idea of ... c6–c5 and ... d5–d4. In the event of 13 ed cd 14 g4 it is best to continue 14 ... e6 15 h4 h5 16 ♕f4 ♕b6 with equality (Timman–Sax, Niksic 1983).

(c) 11 ... ♗e6 12 ♗xg7 ♔xg7 13 ed (worth considering is 13 e5 ♘d7: A. Sokolov–Shneider, Lvov 1984) 13 ... cd 14 g4 ♕c7 15 ♕d4 ♔g8 16 ♗h3?! ♖ab8 17 g5 ♘h5 18 ♗g4 ♘f4 19 ♖he1 ♖fc8 20 ♖e5 ♕b7! and Black took the initiative (Solozhenkin–Nesis, Leningrad 1984).

(d) 11 ... ♗xh6 12 ♕xh6 ♕b6! 13 e5 ♘d7 14 h4 ♘xe5 15 h5 ♗f5 16 g4 f6! 17 ♕f4 ♖ab8, when Black's position is to be preferred (Lyutsko–Shabalov, USSR 1983).

(e) 11 ... e6 12 h4 ♗h8!? 13 h5?! (in the event of 13 ♗xf8 ♕xf8 Black has adequate compensation for the loss of material; play is sharp after 13 g4) 13 ... ♘xh5 14 ♗xf8 ♕xf8 and Black has good prospects (Lobron–Kudrin, New York 1983).

10	...	♘xd5
11	♘xc6	bc
12	♗d4	

Thirty years after the widely-quoted games Ravinsky–Beilin and Stolyar–Beilin (Leningrad 1955), interest in accepting the gambit was re-born. For example: 12 ♘xd5 cd 13 ♕xd5 ♕c7 14 ♕c5 ♕b7 15 b3 ♗f5 16 ♗d3 ♖fc8 with chances for both sides (Blodstein–Petrunko, USSR 1985).

12	...	e5
13	♗c5	♗e6

For a long time this move was played almost automatically. But recently the attention of theoreticians was attracted by the continuation 13 ... ♖e8 14 ♘xd5 cd 15 ♕xd5 (as shown by the game Hazai–Petursson, Tallinn 1981, winning the exchange with 15 ♗b5 does not promise White any advantage: 15 ... ♗e6 16 ♗xe8 ♕xe8 17 ♕a5 ♕c6 18 ♖d3 d4 19 ♖e1 h5!, and Black has a strong and mobile centre in return for the exchange; also good for Black is 15 ... d4 16 ♗xe8 ♕xe8 17 ♔b1 ♗f5 18 ♖c1 ♖c8 19 ♗a3 ♕b5 with more than adequate compensation: Dolmatov–Dorfman, Yerevan 1982) 15 ... ♕xd5 16 ♖xd5 ♗e6 17 ♖d3 ♗xa2 18 ♖a3! ♗h6+ 19 ♗e3 ♗xe3+ 20 ♖xe3 with a small advantage to White (Stoica–Grunberg, Romanian Ch. 1983).

14	♘e4	♖b8

A comparatively new continuation. The usual 14 ... ♖e8 guarantees White the better game. For example: 15 h4 h6 16 g4 ♘f6 17 ♕c3 ♗d5 18 h5 g5 19 ♕a3 ♕c7 20 ♗a6 (Psakhis–Vasyukov, USSR Ch. 1980/81), or 15 ♗c4 ♕c7 16 g4 ♖ed8 17 ♕e1 ♘f4 18 ♗d6 ♕b6 19 ♗xe6 ♘xe6 20 ♗e7 (Poleshchuk–Nesis, corr. 1977/78).

15	c4	

The complications do not turn out in White's favour after 15 g4 f5 16 gf gf 17 ♖g1 fe 18 ♕h6 ♕f6 19 ♖xg7+ ♕xg7 20 ♕xe6+ (Black gets the advantage after 20 ♗xf8 ♔xf8 21 ♕xe6 ♕g5+ 22 ♖d2 ♖d8: Foigel–Yurtaev, USSR 1981) 20 ... ♔h8! 21 ♗xf8 ♕g5+ 22 ♔b1 ♖xf8 23 ♕xc6 ♘e3 24 ♖e1 ♘xf1 25 ♖xf1 ef 26

♕e4 f2! and Black won (Dolmatov–A. Schneider, Budapest 1982).

Black also gets a good game after 15 h4. For example: 15 ...
f5 16 ♘g5 e4! 17 ♗d4 e3 18 ♕d3 ♕d7 19 a3?! f4! (see Game 39;
Zagrebelny–Khalifman), or 15 ... h6 16 g4 ♕c7 17 h5 g5 18 ♗c4
♖fd8 19 ♕f2 a5! (Sigurjonsson–Mestel, Thessaloniki Ol. 1984).
Also interesting is 15 ... ♕c7!? 16 h5 ♖fd8 17 hg ♘b4! 18 gf+
♗xf7 19 ♗d6 ♘xa2+ 20 ♔b1 ♕b6 21 c4 ♖xd6! (Jasnikowski–
Perenyi, Hungary 1984).

15 ...   ♖e8 *(99)*

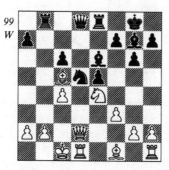

99
W

16 ♔b1

Apparently more accurate is 16 g4 ♕c8 17 ♘d6 ♕a6 18 b3 ♘f6
19 ♘xe8 ♖xe8 20 g5! (Short–Speelman, Baku 1983). True, in this
line Black has the manoeuvre 16 ... ♘b6 17 ♕c2 ♘d7, and now
neither 18 ♗d6 ♖b7 18 ♗d3 ♕a5 (Õim–Reshko, corr. 1983/84),
nor 18 h4 ♕a5 19 ♗a3 ♘f6 (Oll–Gufeld, Tbilisi 1983), promises
White anything special, but worth considering is 17 ♗d6!.

16 ...   ♘b6
17 ♕e1   ♘d7
18 ♗d6   f5!

This is basically a new idea in this variation. For White's dark-
squared bishop Black is prepared to give up not his king's rook
but his queen's rook.

19 ♗xb8   ♕xb8
20 ♘g5   e4
21 ♖d2   ♘c5!

Black has obtained a lot of play for his pieces in compensation
for the exchange. For example, after 22 ♘xe6 ♖xe6 his threats
would become exceedingly dangerous. The price of each move in
such situations is very high.

22   ♕e3   f4!?

Not concerned about considerable loss of material, Black endeavours to bring his light-squared bishop into the game.

23   ♕xc5   e3 *(100)*

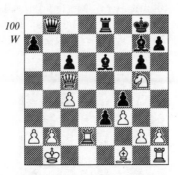

100
W

An interesting position has arisen. White has an extra rook, but Black's pieces are placed very aggresively. The defended passed pawn on e3 makes the situation particularly dynamic.

24   ♖d4

The only correct decision. The dark-squared bishop is worth more than the rook. In the event of 24 ♖e2 ♖d8! Black's attack would become irresistible.

24   ...   ♗f5+

25   ♘e4

Again the only move. After 25 ♔c1 e2 26 ♗xe2 ♖xe2 White is defenceless. But now Black not only regains his rook, he also wins the exchange.

25   ...   ♗xd4

It was still not too late for Black to get carried away with his attack: 25 ... ♖d8 26 ♖xd8+ ♕xd8, and after 27 a3! to be no better off than when he started.

26   ♕xd4   ♖d8

27   ♕c3

White would lose after 27 ♕c5, in view of 27 ... ♖d1+ 28 ♔c2 ♖d2+.

27   ...   ♖d1+

28   ♔c2   e2

29   ♗xe2   ♖xh1

30   c5! *(101)*

The players have exchanged roles. Now it is Black who has a

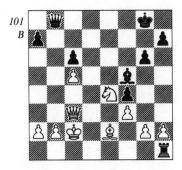

lead in material, but his forces are disconnected and the position of his monarch causes him some anxiety.

30	...	h5
31	♕f6!	

Now, in view of the threat 32 ♗c4+, Black could have reconciled himself to a draw after 31 ... ♕b4, but he prefers to continue the struggle in rather surprising fashion — by 'blundering' his bishop away.

31	...	♕e8!?

This looks like a most awful blunder.

32	♗c4+	♚h7
33	♕xf5	gf
34	♘f6+	♚g6
35	♘xe8	

This dramatic duel has developed throughout in such a way that the player having a lead in material has been forced to fight for a draw. The black rook, having dozed off behind enemy lines, suddenly becomes extremely active. Nimzowitsch once noted that when a piece becomes free again after languishing out of play for a long time, its only aim is to destroy everything in its path.

35	...	♖xh2
36	♗f1	♖h1
37	♗d3	♖g1
38	b4	♖xg2+

Black's passed h-pawn, fenced off from the white pieces by the three pawns on the f-file, is a source of great danger. White needs to play very accurately.

39	♚c3	a6!?

Attempting at the cost of the a-pawn to slow down the white

pawns: 40 ♗xa6 h4 etc. But White is again on his guard.

	40	a4

This endgame is one that requires calculation, and White dare not waste a single tempo.

	40	...	h4
	41	b5	ab
	42	ab	h3
	43	b6! *(102)*	

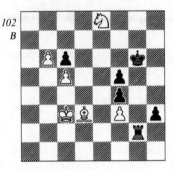

The final subtlety. In the event of the careless 43 bc ♖a2!, or 43 ♗f1 ♖g3!, Black would again have had real winning chances.

	43	...	h2
	44	b7	h1 (♛)
	45	b8 (♛)	

By metamorphosis the material on the board has changed yet again. In such cases the winning side is often the one that is first to give a check. Unfortunately for Black, on this occasion he only has perpetual check, but considering the fluctuating nature of this encounter there is no way you could call such an outcome peaceful.

	45	...	♛c1+
	46	♔d4	♛e3+

Drawn.

Game No. 34
Nunn–Khalifman
Wijk aan Zee 1991

1	e4	c5
2	♘f3	d6
3	d4	cd
4	♘xd4	♘f6

5	♘c3	g6
6	♗e3	♗g7
7	f3	0–0
8	♕d2	♘c6
9	♗c4	♗d7
10	h4	♖c8
11	♗b3	♘e5
12	0–0–0	♘c4
13	♗xc4	♖xc4
14	h5	♘xh5
15	g4	♘f6

This variation has been the subject of intense interest for a quarter of a century, and a great deal has been written about this position. As yet there has been no conclusive assessment, even though testing has been carried out at the very highest level.

16 ♘b3

The most fashionable move in recent games. Also very interesting is the continuation 16 e5 de 17 ♘b3 ♖c6 18 ♗c5 (an idea suggested by Miles). The game Wibe–Nesis, corr. Ol. 1989/91, mentioned in the introduction, continued in far from standard fashion: 18 ... h6!? 19 ♖xh6!? b6 20 ♖h4 bc 21 ♕h2 ♖e8 22 ♖h1 ♔f8 23 ♖h8+ ♘g8 24 ♖h7 g5! 25 ♘xc5 ♗c8 26 ♖xg7 ♔xg7 27 ♕xe5+ ♔f8 28 ♖h7 ♖g6 29 ♘e4 f6 and Black beat off the attack.

16	...	♖e8!
17	♗h6	♗h8
18	♗g5	♕c8

A new continuation. In the game V. Dimitrov–Tolnai, Stara Zagora 1990, Black first sacrificed the exchange — 18 ... ♖xc3 19 bc — and only then continued 19 ... ♕c8; after 20 ♖h4 ♗e6 21 ♖dh1 the position was unclear, but White here had the strong move 20 e5!, and so Black is first to diverge from this line.

19 ♕h2

In the event of 19 ♖h4 Black has the opportunity to return to the game Dimitrov–Tolnai. A sharp position would arise after 19 e5!? ♘xg4 20 fg ♗xg4 21 ed ed (21 ... ♗xd1!? 22 d7) 22 ♖de1.

19 ... ♗e6

Worth considering was the continuation 19 ... ♖xc3!? 20 bc ♗e6 21 ♖d3 ♕c4, with roughly equal chances.

20 ♖d3! *(103)*

In such positions there is no point in winning back the pawn: after 20 ♗xf6 ♗xf6 21 ♕xh7+ ♔f8 the powerful dark-squared bishop guarantees Black the advantage. But the move in the game sets Black difficult problems. The threat is 21 e5 de 22 ♘d2 and 23 ♘e4.

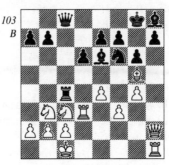

                    20   ...   h5!
Black is planning to take the pawn on g4 with his knight, after which he will have three pawns for his piece, at the same time neutralising White's initiative on the kingside.
                    21   gh
Nothing good for White is promised by playing 21 ♗xf6 ♗xf6 22 gh g5!.

21	...	♘xh5
22	♕g2	♗xc3
23	bc	♖xc3
24	♖xc3	

It would be bad to play 24 ♔b2 ♖xd3 25 cd ♗xb3 26 ab ♕c5 27 ♖xh5, because of 27 ... ♖c8!.

24	...	♕xc3
25	♖xh5	*(104)*
25	...	♗xb3

The white rook cannot be captured, because of 26 ♗f6+.

26	ab	♕a1+
27	♔d2	♖c8

Worse was 27 ... ♕d4+ 28 ♔e2 ♖c8, in view of 29 c4! ♕b2+ 30 ♗d2 ♕xb3 31 ♖h8+! ♔xh8 32 ♕h3+ ♔g7 33 ♕xc8 with a better position for White.
                    28   ♖h2
Defending against the threat of 27 ... ♖xc2+ and 28 ... ♕a2+.

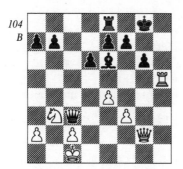

| 28 | ... | ♕d4+ |
| 29 | ♔c1 | *(105)* |

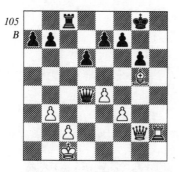

An attempt to deviate from perpetual check would be very risky: 29 ♔e1 ♕a1+ 30 ♔e2 ♖xc2+ 31 ♗d2 ♕a6+.

29	...	♕a1+
30	♔d2	♕d4+
31	♔c1	Drawn.

Game No. 35
Kindermann–Kir. Georgiev
Dortmund 1991

1	e4	c5
2	♘f3	d6
3	d4	cd
4	♘xd4	♘f6
5	♘c3	g6
6	♗e3	♗g7
7	f3	♘c6

8	♗c4	0–0
9	♕d2	♗d7
10	0–0–0	♘e5
11	♗b3	♖c8
12	♗g5	

It looks more logical to play this move after a preliminary 12 h4 h5.

| 12 | ... | ♘c4!? |

Complying with White's plans. Worth considering was 12 ... ♖c5 and now 13 h4!? leads after 13 ... h5 14 f4 ♘c4 15 15 ♕d3 ♘g4 16 ♗xc4 ♘f2 17 ♕e2 ♘xh1 18 ♗b3 to a sharp but rather well-studied position. The game Adams–Tiviakov, Oakham 1990, continued: 18 ... a5 19 f5 a4 20 ♗d5 ♕e8 with quite good chances for Black.

Also possible is 12 ... ♕a5!? 13 ♔b1 ♖c5.

| 13 | ♗xc4 | ♖xc4 |
| 14 | e5 | |

Unpleasant for Black is 14 ♖he1!, when it is not easy for him to get any active play.

| 14 | ... | de |
| 15 | ♘de2 | (106) |

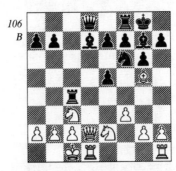

This move is the point of White's plan: Black cannot avoid losing the exchange. But two strong bishops and a pawn give him entirely adequate compensation.

Previously 15 ♘b3 had been played here.

15	...	♖c7
16	♗xf6	ef
17	♘b5	♗f5!
18	♘xc7	♕xc7

19	♘c3	♖c8
20	♔b1	♗e6
21	♘e4	♕c4

A rather hasty move. Worth considering was 21 ... h6 followed by 22 ... f5.

22	b3	♕c6
23	c4	f5
24	♘g5	♗xc4 *(107)*

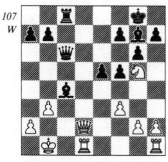

25 ♖c1!

Not, of course, 25 bc e4!, with an irresistible attack for Black. But now White seizes the initiative.

25	...	♕b5
26	♖hd1	e4
27	♖xc4	♖xc4
28	♕d8+	♗f8 *(108)*

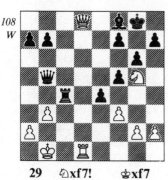

29	♘xf7!	♔xf7
30	♖d7+	♔g8
31	♕e8	

Black's position gives him cause for serious concern. White

threatens both 32 ♕f7+ with mate, and 32 ♖g7+ winning the queen. Fortunately for Black he has perpetual check.

31	...	♖c1+!
32	♔xc1	♕c5+
33	♔b2	♕f2+
34	♔c3	♕e3+
35	♔c2	♕c5+!
36	♔b2	

White achieves nothing with 36 ♔d1, because of 36 ... ♕g1+ 37 ♔e2 ♕xg2+ 38 ♔e3 ♕xf3+ 39 ♔d4 ♕d3+ 40 ♔e5 ♕c3+ 41 ♔e6 ♕c6+.

36	...	♕f2+
37	♔c3	Drawn.

Game No. 36
Monin–Rusakov
17th USSR Corr. Ch. 1986/88

1	e4	c5
2	♘f3	d6
3	d4	cd
4	♘xd4	♘f6
5	♘c3	a6
6	♗g5	e6
7	f4	♗e7
8	♕f3	♕c7
9	0–0–0	h6!

In the event of a different move order — 9 ... ♘bd7 10 ♗d3 h6 — White has the possibility of continuing 11 h4!? with sharp play. For example, 11 ... ♘c5 12 f5 ♘xd3+ 13 ♕xd3 ♗d7 (stronger is 13 ... hg!?) 14 fe fe 15 e5! de 16 ♕g6+ ♔f8 17 ♗xf6 ♗xf6 18 ♖hf1 ♗c8 19 ♖xf6+ gf 20 ♕xf6+ ♔g8 21 ♘f5 ef 22 ♖d8+ resigns (Carleton–Marcinkiewicz, corr. 1981).

10	♗h4	♘bd7
11	♗d3	g5
12	e5	gh
13	ef	♘xf6
14	f5	

An unclear position would also be reached after 14 ♖he1 ♗d7 15 ♕f2 0–0–0 16 ♘f5 ♗c6 17 ♕a7 ♖he8 (analysis by Minic).

| 14 | ... | e5 |

15	♘de2	♗d7
16	♗e4 *(109)*	

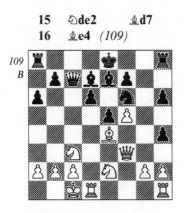

| 16 | ... | ♗c6 |

Worth considering is Lepeshkin's suggestion 16 ... d5!, when the opening of diagonals gives Black quite good counter-chances.

17	♘d5	♗xd5
18	♗xd5	♖c8
19	♘c3	

The white pieces have successfully erected a blockade on the light squares.

19	...	b5
20	♗b7?! *(110)*	

The move recommended by *ECO* — 20 ♗b3 — would lead to a solid advantage for White, but now Black finds an ingenious move which gives him chances.

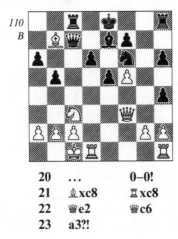

20	...	0–0!
21	♗xc8	♖xc8
22	♕e2	♕c6
23	a3?!	

This natural move turned out not to be the best. White should have played 23 ♖he1! d5 24 ♕xe5 b4 25 ♕xe7 bc 26 ♕a3.

23	...	e4!
24	♖d4	d5
25	♖hd1	♗xa3
26	♘xd5	♘xd5
27	♖xd5	*(111)* Drawn.

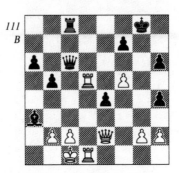

111 B

After 27 ... ♗xb2+ 28 ♔xb2 ♕c3+ 29 ♔a2 ♕a5+ 30 ♔b1 ♕b4+ perpetual check is unavoidable (analysis by Barash).

Game No. 37
Wahls–Hübner
W. Germany 1989

1	e4	c5
2	♘f3	♘c6
3	d4	cd
4	♘xd4	♘f6
5	♘c3	d6
6	♗c4	e6
7	♗e3	a6
8	♕e2	♕c7

Flank operations with 8 ... ♘a5 9 ♗d3 b5 would be refuted by 10 b4!, when if 10 ... ♘b7 then 11 0–0 followed by 12 a4.

9	♗b3	♗e7
10	0–0–0	0–0

The game takes on quite a different appearance in the event of 10 ... ♗d7 11 g4 ♘xd4 12 ♖xd4 ♗c6 13 g5 ♘d7 14 f4 ♘c5 15 ♖hd1. Weaker is 10 ... b5, after which 11 ♘xc6 ♕xc6 12 ♗d4

♗d7 (on 12 ... 0–0 there follows 13 ♘d5!) 13 ♖he1 is unpleasant for Black.

11   g4

Also worth considering is 11 f4, in reply to which Black plays 11 ... ♘xd4 12 ♖xd4 b5 13 ♖f1 ♖b8 14 a3 ♗d7 15 f5 ef 16 ef a5 with a good game (analysis by Nikitin).

11   ...   ♘xd4
12   ♖xd4

On 12 ♗xd4, possible is 12 ... e5 13 ♗e3 ♗xg4 14 f3 ♗e6, when White has no compensation at all for the loss of a pawn.

12   ...   b5

Here after 12 ... e5 White would play 13 ♖c4, and on 12 ... ♘d7 White gets an attack with 13 g5 ♘c5 14 e5! de 15 ♖h4.

13   g5   ♘d7
14   f4

In this situation White achieves nothing by playing 14 e5 de 15 ♖h4, because of 15 ... ♖d8 16 ♕h5 ♘f8. The line 14 ♖g1 ♘c5 15 e5 was considered in Game 12; Szmetan–G. Garcia.

14   ...   ♘c5 *(112)*

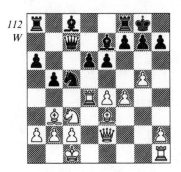

15   f5!

Worse for White is 15 h4 ♗d7 16 g6 a5! with a very nasty pawn offensive.

15   ...   ef
16   ♗d5

Tempting is 16 ♘d5 ♕d8 17 e5, but after 17 ... ♘xb3+ 18 ab de! 19 ♘f6+ ♗xf6 20 ♖xd8 ♗xd8 Black gets adequate compensation for his queen.

16   ...   ♖b8
17   ef   b4!

Analysis shows that after 17 ... ♗xf5 18 ♖f1 White's attack would have been very strong.

The following continuations come into consideration: 18 ... ♗g6 19 h4 ♕d7 20 ♕f3, and there is no defence against 21 h5; 18 ... g6 19 ♖xf5 gf 20 ♕h5, followed by 21 ♖h4; 18 ... ♗e6 19 ♕h5 ♕d7 20 ♖df4, and the f7-square falls; and 18 ... ♕d7 19 ♖df4 ♗h3 20 ♕h5.

18	**g6!**	**hg**
19	**fg**	**♗e6**
20	**♗xe6**	**♘xe6**
21	**♘d5**	

White achieves nothing with 21 ♕h5 fg 22 ♕d5 bc 23 ♕xe6+ ♖f7.

21	**...**	**♘xd4**
22	**♗xd4**	**♗g5+**
23	**♔b1**	**♕b7** *(113)*

Black is hanging on by a thread, but all the same his position is entirely defensible.

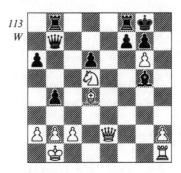

113
W

24	**♕h5**	**♗h6**
25	**♘f6+**	

25 ♖g1 fg 26 ♕xg6 leads after 26 ... ♕xd5 27 ♗xg7 ♖f1+ 28 ♖xf1 ♗xg7 to a win for Black.

25	**...**	**gf**
26	**♖g1**	**fg**
27	**♕xh6**	**♖f7**
28	**b3!**	

White does not hurry. Weaker was 28 ♖xg6+ ♖g7, when White cannot play 29 ♗xf6 because of 29 ... ♕h1+.

28	**...**	**♖c8!**

The idea behind this move is that after 29 ♖xg6+ ♖g7 30 ♗xf6 ♕h1+ 31 ♔b2 Black has the tactical trick 31 ... ♖xc2+! 32 ♔xc2 ♕e4+.

29	**h4!**	

With the threat of 30 h5.

29	...	♖h7
30	♖xg6+	♖g7
31	h5	♕h1+
32	♔b2 *(114)*	

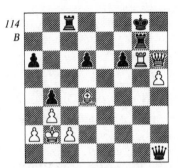

Now Black demolishes the pawn cover protecting the white king and gets a draw by perpetual check.

32	...	♖xc2+
33	♔xc2	♕e4+
34	♔c1	♕e1+
35	♔b2	♕e2+
36	♔c1	♕e1+

Drawn.

Game No. 38
Bronstein–Suetin
Moscow 1982

1	e4	c5
2	♘f3	e6
3	d4	cd
4	♘xd4	a6
5	♗d3	♗c5
6	♘b3	♗b6

This continuation is met more rarely than 6 ... ♗a7. White usually implements the same plan, involving the moves ♕e2 and

♗e3. After an exchange of dark-squared bishops on e3 play transposes to the variation with 6 ... ♗a7. The difference between the moves 6 ... ♗b6 and 6 ... ♗a7 is that after 6 ... ♗b6 Black can refrain from exchanging bishops on e3, not fearing a capture on b6. On the other hand, the position of the bishop on b6 makes it difficult for Black to play ... b7–b5, which is important in some variations.

	7	♕e2	♘c6
	8	♗e3	♘f6?!

Better is 8 ... ♗xe3 at once, transposing to the usual variations. But now 9 ♗xb6 ♕xb6 10 e5 ♘d5 11 ♘1d2 ♘f4 12 ♕e4 ♕b4 13 ♗c4 ♘g6 14 c3 ♕e7 15 f4 gives White an undoubted advantage (Timman–Djuric, Sarajevo 1984).

	9	♘c3	d6
	10	f4	♗xe3
	11	♕xe3	♕c7

The queen moves off the d-file, evading the potential threat of e4–e5.

	12	0–0–0	0–0
	13	♕h3	

This interesting continuation was adopted for the first time in the present game.

White prepares to play 14 g4 without sacrificing a pawn (as occurred in Game 14; Kengis–Nevednichy). Also frequently played in this position is the move 13 ♖hg1 (see Game 57; Spassky–Capelan).

	13	...	b5
	14	g4	♘b4

Black defends with great care. In the event of 14 ... b4 15 g5 ♘d7 16 ♘d5 ♕d8 17 e5 White would have an irresistible attack.

	15	g5	♘xd3+
	16	♖xd3	♘e8

The game has reached a typical Sicilian position. Now White needs to solve his main task: whether to prevent the knight on c3 from being attacked by ... b5–b4 (with the move 17 a3) or to attack the main weakness in Black's position – the h7-square — in order not to slacken the pace of his attack. He chooses the second option.

	17	f5	

Also worth considering was the immediate 17 ♕h4. After 17 ...

f6 18 ♖h3 g6 19 gf ♘xf6 20 ♖hg1 White has some advantage.

17 ... b4 *(115)*

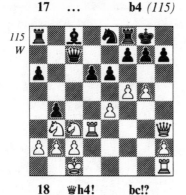

18 ♕h4! bc!?

Bronstein considers this to be an exceptionally brave decision.

It would appear that it was possible to play 18 ... f6 (19 ♖h3 g6 20 fg bc 21 gh+ ♔h8, and White's attack is beaten off). However, after 18 ... f6 19 g6 the unfortunate position of the black knight on e8 would mean that White maintains a dangerous initiative.

19 ♖h3

Worth considering was a preliminary 19 ♖xc3, and only then 20 ♖h3.

19 ... cb+
20 ♔b1 f6

The key move, on which Black's entire defence depends. The other way to defend (20 ... h6) would not have helped, in view of 21 f6 e5 22 fg ♗xh3 23 gh! ♘xg7 24 hg ♔xg7 25 ♖g1+.

21 ♕xh7+ ♔f7 *(116)*

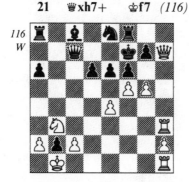

A critical position. White has a strong attack, but Black has an extra piece. Black's task is to bring his light-squared bishop into play as quickly as possible, but for the time being White is bearing down on the black king with all his major pieces.

	22	♖g1	♖g8
	23	♖h6	ef *(117)*

A natural move, but not the strongest. It would have been much more difficult for White to continue his attack after 23 ... ♔f8!, as he would achieve nothing with 24 gf because of 24 ... ef 25 fg+ ♖xg7 26 ♕h8+ ♔f7 27 ♖h7 ♕c3.

Now after the obvious 24 gf Black could still have transposed to the variation examined above with the move 24 ... ♔f8. So Bronstein decided to wreck the position of the black king.

	24	♖xf6+!	♘xf6
	25	gf *(118)*	

Again a very interesting position. Now retreating the king to f8 is dangerous, because of 26 fg+ ♔f7 27 ef, when an extra rook is hardly sufficient to save Black. There is only one way out — to give back the material.

	25	...	♔xf6

26	♕xg8	♗b7
27	♕h7	♗xe4
28	♕g6+	♔e5
29	♕g3+	Drawn.

The players agreed to a draw, in view of the variation 29 ... ♔f6 30 ♕g5+ ♔e5 31 ♕d2 (the only way to play for a win) 31 ... ♕xc2+ 32 ♕xc2 ♗xc2+ 33 ♔xc2 ♖h8 34 ♔xb2 ♖xh2+ 35 ♔c3 ♖xa2 36 ♖xg7.

7   Enticement

With the aid of this tactical method a piece (or pawn) is compelled to occupy a particular square, as a result of which the attacking side gets definite chances to achieve its goal.

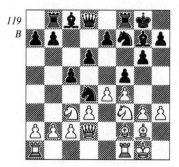

*119
B*

This position arose in the game Grigoriev–Panikovsky, Kurgan 1972, in which the Closed Variation of the Sicilian Defence was played.

11	...	fe
12	♘xd4	

Otherwise White loses a pawn after 12 ... ♘xf3+; now after 12 ... cd 13 ♘xe4 his position would be quite in order. But White was in for a nasty surprise.

12	...	e3!!

The black pawn sacrifices itself, but this entices one of the white pieces onto the e3-square, after which the knight on d4 will be captured by the pawn and White's pieces will be forked.

White resigned.

Game No. 39
Zagrebelny–Khalifman
Sochi 1984

1	e4	c5
2	♘f3	d6
3	d4	cd
4	♘xd4	♘f6
5	♘c3	g6
6	♗e3	♗g7
7	f3	0-0
8	♕d2	♘c6
9	0-0-0	

The modern way of playing this variation usually involves a preliminary 9 ♗c4, in order to avoid the continuation chosen in this game.

| | 9 | ... | d5!? |

Konstantinopolsky's variation, which leads to a sharp and interesting struggle.

10	ed	♘xd5
11	♘xc6	bc
12	♗d4	e5
13	♗c5	♗e6
14	♘e4	♖b8
15	h4?!	

This move makes an unfavourable impression at first glance, and the subsequent course of the game confirms this impression. Undoubtedly the strongest move is 15 c4 (see Game 33; Kosenkov–Nesis).

| | 15 | ... | f5 |

Also not bad is 15 ... h6; and 15 ... ♕c7 has also been tried.

| 16 | ♘g5 *(120)* |

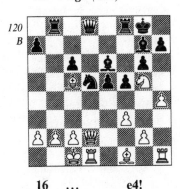

| | 16 | ... | e4! |

It turns out that the bishop on e6 cannot be captured, because of 16 ... ♗xb2+ 17 ♔b1 ♘c3+.

	17	♗d4

On 17 c3 there follows 17 ... ♕a5 18 ♗xf8 ♕xa2.

	17	...	e3
	18	♕d3	♕d7
	19	a3	

Forestalling the manoeuvre ... ♘d5–b4.

	19	...	f4
	20	♘xe6	♕xe6
	21	♗xg7	♔xg7
	22	♕d4+	♔h6
	23	♗d3	

Worth considering was 23 ♗c4.

	23	...	c5
	24	♕c4 *(121)*	

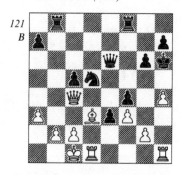

	24	...	♖xb2!

The white king is enticed onto the b2-square.

	25	h5	

In the event of 25 ♔xb2 ♕e5+ 26 c3 ♖b8+ 27 ♔c1 (if 27 ♔c2 then 27 ... e2) 27 ... ♘xc3 28 ♖de1 ♘a4 White is defenceless.

	25	...	♖fb8
	26	hg+	♔g7
	27	c3	

White declines to play the tempting 27 ♖xh7+, in order to keep a rook on the back rank.

	27	...	e2
	28	♗e4	ed(♕)+
	29	♖xd1 *(122)*	

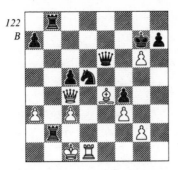

122
B

The impression is that White has obtained some counter-chances, but Black has an ingenious tactical trick.

> 29 ... 🜚b1+‼

Thanks to this move, the white bishop is 'removed' from its official post and the black queen tears into White's position.

> 30 ♗xb1 ♛e3+
> 31 ♚c2 ♛f2+
> 32 ♚d3 🜚e8
> 33 ♛a2 *(123)*

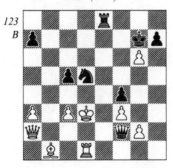

123
B

> 33 ... c4+!

Another enticement of the white king!

> 34 ♚xc4 ♛xa2+
> 35 ♗xa2 ♞e3+

White resigned.

Game No. 40
Zakic–Cvetkovic
Aosta 1989

> 1 e4 c5

2	♘f3	e6
3	d4	cd
4	♘xd4	♘f6
5	♘c3	d6
6	g4	♘c6
7	g5	♘d7
8	♗e3	♗e7
9	h4	0-0

A courageous move: Black is ready to repel his opponent's attack.

10 ♕h5

Usually White plays a 'shorter' move with the queen: 10 ♕e2. After 10 ... ♘xd4 11 ♗xd4 a6 12 0-0-0 b5 13 a3 ♖b8 14 f4 ♖e8 15 ♕h2 (also possible is 15 ♕h5) the tension mounts in typical Sicilian fashion: 15 ... b4!? (but not 15 ... ♕a5?! 16 g6! fg 17 h5 ♗f8 18 hg h6 19 f5 b4 20 ♕h5! — threatening 21 f6 and f7+ — 20 ... ♕d8 21 fe ♘f6 22 ♗xf6 ♕xf6 23 ♘d5 ♕d8 24 ab with a big advantage to White: Bellin–Stohl, Oberwart 1989) 16 ab ♖xb4 17 g6 fg 18 h5 e5 19 hg h6 20 fe ♗g5+ with an unclear position.

10	...	♖e8
11	0-0-0	a6
12	f4	♗f8

Worth considering was 12 ... ♘xd4.

13 f5!? ef? (124)

This move was played in expectation of 14 ♘xf5 ♘de5! (but not 14 ... g6?! 15 ♘h6+ ♗xh6 16 ♕xh6 ♘de5 17 ♘d5). But Black should have played 13 ... ♘de5! at once, when his defensive resources would have been quite considerable.

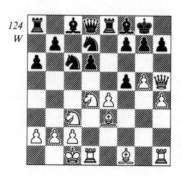

*124
W*

	14	♕xf7+!!

A bolt from the blue: the black king is enticed into a very strong attack.

	14	...	♔xf7

14 ... ♔h8 is hopeless, because of 15 ♗c4.

	15	♗c4+	♖e6

It would be mate in one after either 15 ... ♔e7 16 ♘xf5 mate, or 15 ... ♔g6 16 h5 mate. Black gets nowhere with 15 ... d5, because of 16 ♗xd5+ ♖e6 17 ♘xe6 ♕a5 18 ♘c7+ ♔e7 19 ♘xa8, when White has a decisive advantage.

	16	♘xe6	♕a5

Of course, Black cannot play 16 ... ♕e7, in view of 17 ♘c7+ ♔g6 18 h5 mate.

	17	♘c7+	♔e7

If 17 ... d5 then 18 ♖xd5 wins immediately.

	18	♘3d5+	♔d8
	19	♘e6+	♔e8
	20	♗d2!	

White prefers to continue his attack rather than capture the black rook on a8.

	20	...	♕a4
	21	♗b3	♕xe4
	22	♖he1!	♖b8

If the queen were to move away (22 ... ♕xh4) Black would be mated: 23 ♘ec7++ ♔f7 24 ♘f4+ d5 25 ♗xd5 mate.

	23	♖xe4	fe
	24	♖f1!	♘ce5

Black takes control of the f7-square.

| | 25 | ♗b4 | |

Aiming at the pawn on d6.

	25	...	♘f3
	26	♘dc7+	♔e7
	27	♖d1	♘c5
	28	♘xc5	a5

On 28 ... dc there would follow 29 ♗xc5 mate.

	29	♘5a6	ab
	30	♘xb8	♘xh4
	31	♘b5	♗g4
	32	♖xd6	e3
	33	♖b6	e2

34 ♖xb7+ Black resigned.

Black gave up without waiting for the finish: 34 ... ♔e8 35
♗f7+ ♔d8 36 ♘c6+ ♔c8 37 ♖c7 mate.

8 Deflection

The essence of this tactical method is that, as a result of a threat, sacrifice or other diversionary tactic, a piece or pawn belonging to one's opponent is forced to move away and allow access to an important square or file.

In the game Beni–Schwarzbach, Vienna 1969, White played the Sozin Attack, sacrificed a rook and obtained the following position:

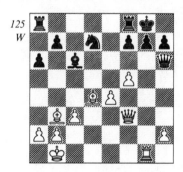

125 W

White's main task is to eliminate the piece defending the g7-square, and to do this he doesn't flinch from sacrificing his queen!

> **21 ♕h3!! ♕xh3**

There is no other move, but now the black queen is diverted from the defence of the king.

> **22 ♖xg7+ ♔h8**
> **23 ♖xf7+ ♔g8**
> **24 ♖g7+**

And mate is inevitable (24 ... ♔h8 25 ♖g8 mate).

Game No. 41
Zagorovsky–Mikhailov
11th Corr. Ch. 1983/85

1	e4	c5
2	♘f3	d6
3	d4	cd
4	♘xd4	♘f6
5	♘c3	g6
6	♗e3	♗g7
7	f3	♘c6
8	♕d2	♗d7

Black does not hurry to castle, and so avoids the standard position arising after 8 ... 0–0 9 ♗c4 ♗d7 10 h4 etc.

9	0–0–0	♖c8
10	♔b1	

The game Yudovich–Averbakh, Moscow 1964, continued: 10 g4 0–0 11 h4 ♘xd4 12 ♗xd4 ♕a5 13 ♔b1 e5 14 ♗e3 ♗e6 15 ♘d5 ♕xd2 16 ♘xf6+ ♗xf6 17 ♖xd2 ♗e7 with an equal ending.

10	...	♘e5
11	g4	a6
12	h4	h5

The standard plan of blocking the white h-pawn, but the difference here is that Black has not yet castled and White's bishop is on its original square instead of b3.

13	g5	♘h7
14	♗e2	0–0
15	♘b3	b5
16	♗d4	♘c4
17	♗xc4	bc
18	♗xg7	♔xg7
19	♕d4+	

In the event of 19 ♘d4 Black would get counterplay with 19 ... ♕a5!.

19	...	♔g8
20	♘d2	♗e6
21	♘f1	f6 *(126)*

A serious weakening, but White's threat of storming the black king's fortress with the f-pawn forces Black to take action.

22	gf	♖xf6
23	e5	

White does not lose time in defending his f-pawn and begins a well-calculated tactical operation.

23	...	♖xf3

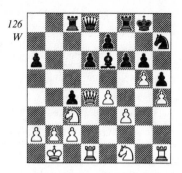

24	♕e4	♗g4
25	♘h2!	

Now 25 ... ♖xc3 would be insufficient, because of 26 ♘xg4.

25	...	♖f5
26	♘xg4	hg
27	ed	ed
28	h5!	

The h-pawn manages nonetheless to inflict the decisive wound.

28	...	♕e8

On 28 ... ♘g5 sufficient is the simple 29 ♕xg4, and on 28 ... ♘f6, as Zagorovsky pointed out, decisive is 29 ♕e6+ ♔g7 30 hg ♔xg6 31 ♖dg1! ♖g5 32 ♘e4.

29	hg	♕xg6 *(127)*

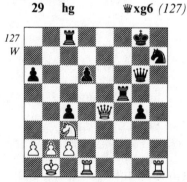

Now White lands a tactical punch which makes use of the idea of deflection and also the fact that Black's two undefended rooks on f5 and c8 are on the same diagonal.

30	♖xd6!	♕xd6
31	♕xg4+	♘g5
32	♕xf5	♖c5

33	♕f2

Despite the considerable degree of simplification, the position of Black's king is still extremely perilous, not to mention the fact that Black is a pawn down.

33	...	♖e5
34	a3	♔g7
35	♕h4	♕c6
36	♖g1	♔g6
37	♘e4!	♕d5

And now there follows a textbook example of how to transpose to a pawn ending in order to profit from a lead in material.

The result is already quite clear.

38	♖xg5+	♖xg5
39	♕xg5+	♕xg5
40	♘xg5	♔xg5
41	♔c1	Black resigned.

Game No. 42
Ivanovic–Larsen
Niksic 1983

1	e4	c5
2	♘f3	♘c6
3	♘c3	d6
4	d4	cd
5	♘xd4	♘f6
6	♗c4	e6
7	♗e3	♗e7
8	♕e2	

"Bravo!", writes Larsen in his notes to this game. The point is that he had been preparing for many years to play Black against this system, the so-called Velimirovic Attack, which since 1966 had been feared throughout the chess world. Finally, Larsen had his chance — this was the last round of an extremely strong international tournament in Niksic, and in order to finish second overall (Kasparov was first) Larsen needed to win.

8	...	a6
9	♗b3	0–0
10	0–0–0	♕c7
11	♖hg1	♘d7

In the 'Niksic-78' tournament, Ivanovic, playing Black against the inventor of this system, Velimirovic, decided firstly to eliminate the bishop on b3 by playing 11 ... ♘a5, but after 12 g4 b5 13 g5 ♘xb3+ 14 ab ♘d7 15 f4 b4 16 ♘f5! ef 17 ♘d5 he came under very strong attack and White won fairly easily: 17 ... ♛d8 18 ef ♖e8 19 g6 fg 20 fg h6 21 ♛c4 ♔h8 22 ♗d4 ♗f8 23 ♘c7 ♘c5 24 ♘xa8 ♗e6 25 ♛e2 ♛xa8 26 ♛h5 ♔g8 27 ♗xc5 dc 28 f5 ♗d5 29 f6 ♖d8 30 f7+ ♔h8 31 ♛h4 a5 32 ♖ge1 a4 33 ♛xd8! ♛xd8 34 ♖e8 ♛g5+ 35 ♔b1 ♛xg6 36 ♖xf8+ ♔h7 37 ♖h8+ ♔xh8 38 f8(♛)+ ♗g8 39 ♖d8 ♛e6 — after a mass exchange on g8 and the capture of the pawn on a4 the black king is not within the square of the white a-pawn.

12   ♛h5?!

It is difficult to say why White preferred this move to the natural 12 g4, for which see Game 49; Brunner–Hübner. In some variations White may get a mating attack with ♖d1–d3–h3; and after g4 and ♖g1–g3–h3 White's attack develops more quickly than in the usual variations, where in order to transfer his queen to h5 he has firstly to move the g-pawn to g5.

On the other hand, it is not at all clear what White should do after 12 ... ♘f6: go back with the queen to e2, with possible repetition? And 12 ... ♛a5 also seems quite good for Black. But Black preferred to exchange off the knight on d4 in order to exclude the possibility of its being sacrificed on f5 or e6.

12	...	♘xd4
13	♗xd4	b5
14	g4?	(128)

Better was 14 ♖d3 ♘f6 (not, of course, 14 ... g6 because of 15 ♛xh7+ followed by mate) 15 ♛h4, although here too Black seizes the initiative by playing 15 ... e5.

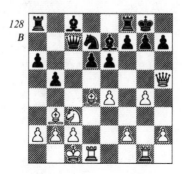

| 14 | ... | ♘f6! |
| 15 | ♕h4 | |

It turns out that after 15 ♕h3 b4 16 g5 ♘e8! Black wins a piece.

15	...	♘xe4
16	g5	♘xc3
17	♗xc3	

It was tempting to play 17 ♗f6, in order on 17 ... ♘xd1 to inflict the decisive blow 18 ♕h6!! But Black has the prosaic reply 17 ... ♘e2+ after which he has time to move his king's rook and play ... ♗f8.

| 17 | ... | e5 |

Black not only closes the a1–h8 diagonal but also brings his light-squared bishop into play.

18	f4	♗f5
19	♖df1	♕c5!
20	fe	de
21	♕e1	

Stronger was 21 ♕g3, although here too Black has the better game after 21 ... e4 22 h4 ♗d6.

| 21 | ... | e4 |
| 22 | h4 | |

If 22 a3 then 22 ... ♗h3 is unpleasant.

| 22 | ... | a5! |
| 23 | ♗xa5 | e3! |

It turns out that 24 a3 would now lead to White's defeat after 24 ... e2 25 ♖f2 ♖xa5 26 ♖xf5 ♕xf5 27 ♕xa5 ♗c5 28 ♖e1 b4! 29 ab ♗e3+ 30 ♔b1 ♕f1.

| 24 | ♗b4 | *(129)* |

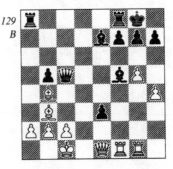

| 24 | ... | ♖xa2!! |

The black queen cannot be taken because of 25 ... ♖a1 mate, and it is also mate in one after 25 ♗xa2.

	25	♔b1	♗xc2+!

Another spectacular capture.

	26	♗xc2	

Or 26 ♔xa2 ♗xb3+ 27 ♔xb3 ♕c4+.

	26	...	♕a7
	27	♗xh7+	

Desperation, but it was no use continuing 27 ♗a3 ♗xa3 28 ♔xa2 ♗b4+.

	27	...	♔xh7
	28	♕c3	♗xb4
	29	g6+	fg
	30	♕c6	♖xf1+

White resigned.

Game No. 43
Brodsky–Kramnik
Kherson 1991

1	e4	c5
2	♘f3	♘c6
3	d4	cd
4	♘xd4	♘f6
5	♘c3	e5
6	♘db5	d6
7	♗g5	a6
8	♘a3	b5

The so-called 'Chelyabinsk Variation' (or Pelikan–Sveshnikov System), which has been extremely popular in recent years.

	9	♗xf6	

Also possible is 9 ♘d5 ♗e7 10 ♘xe7 ♘xe7 11 f3 d5 12 ed ♘exd5 13 c4 bc 14 ♘xc4 0–0 15 ♗e2 with slightly better chances for White.

	9	...	gf
	10	♘d5	f5
	11	♗d3	

The continuations 11 ef and 11 g3 offer White fewer prospects.

	11	...	♗e6
	12	♕h5	

If 12 c4 then 12 ... ♕a5+!.

12	...	♖g8
13	0–0–0?	

The start of an adventurous plan. White should have preferred 13 c3 or 13 g3.

13	...	♖xg2
14	f4	♘d4! *(130)*

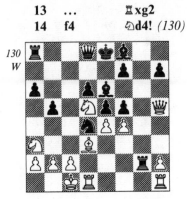

Now on 15 c3 there follows 15 ... ♗xd5 16 ed b4! 17 ♘c4 bc 18 bc ♖c8 19 cd ♕a5 with irresistible mating threats; also bad for White would be 15 ♖hg1 fe! 16 ♖xg2, or 15 ♕h3 ♖g8 16 ♕xh7 ♖g6.

15	♘e3	♖f2
16	ef	♗xa2
17	fe	de
18	♘xb5!? *(131)*	

Can White profit from his centralised pieces? On 18 ... ab he would initiate unclear complications with 19 ♗xb5+ ♔e7 20 f6+. But Kramnik now plays a brilliant combination.

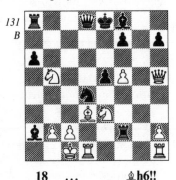

18	...	♗h6!!

The main tactical idea here is the deflection of the white queen.

On 19 ♕xh6 Black plays yet another sacrifice: 19 ... ♖xc2+!, when if 20 ♗xc2 (the bishop is also deflected) then 20 ... ♘e2 mate and if 20 ♘xc2 then 20 ... ♘b3 mate.

19	♖he1	ab
20	♗xb5+	♔e7
21	♕h4+	f6
22	♕xf2	♗f7
23	♗d3	♕b6

Despite his material advantage, White is defenceless.

24	♗e4	♖a2
25	c4	♗xc4
26	♔b1	♕a5
27	♘d5+	♗xd5
28	♕xd4	♖a1+

Of course, not 28 ... ed because of 29 ♗xd5+ and 30 ♗xa2.

29	♔c2	♖xd1

The simplest solution.

30	♕xd1	♕a4+!
31	♔c3	

White resigned, not waiting for 31 ... ♕c4 mate.

Game No. 44
Tal–Larsen
10th game, Bled 1965

1	e4	c5
2	♘f3	♘c6
3	d4	cd
4	♘xd4	e6
5	♘c3	d6
6	♗e3	♘f6
7	f4	♗e7
8	♕f3	

As a consequence of this game this very sharp and uncompromising system became fashionable in tournament play.

8	...	0–0
9	0–0–0	♕c7

Now the immediate 10 g4 would come up against the refutation 10 ... ♘xd4 11 ♖xd4 e5 12 ♖c4 ♗xg4!, but White can go onto the attack after first making his opponent's position worse.

10	♘db5	♕b8

11	g4	a6
12	♘d4	♘xd4
13	♗xd4	b5

Tal considers that Black was obliged to continue 13 ... e5, and he had intended to reply 14 g5. Now an attempt to win the exchange does not work: 14 ... ♗g4 15 ♕g2 ♗xd1? 16 gf ♗xf6 17 ♘d5 ed 18 ♘xf6+ ♔h8 19 ♖g1; but by continuing 15 ... ed (instead of 15 ... ♗xd1) 16 gf dc 17 fe cb+ 18 ♔b1 ♗xd1 Black would retain quite good chances of putting up a successful defence.

14	g5	♘d7
15	♗d3	b4 *(132)*

On 15 ... ♗b7, White would have had the straightforward and very strong 16 ♕h3!.

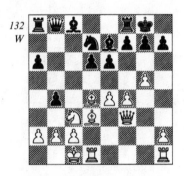

132
W

16	♘d5!?	ed

Black has to take the knight, as otherwise White would play 17 ♘f6+.

17	ed

The piece sacrifice is positional. Black's pieces are bunched up on the queenside (rook on a8, queen on b8, bishop on c8), and it is not so easy for them to come to the aid of their king. Besides, the two white bishops on d3 and d4 are bearing down on the black king. Now the threat is a combination involving the successive sacrifices of these bishops (on h7 and g7), against which it is impossible for Black to defend without making positional concessions. So here Black should have risked playing 17 ... g6!, not fearing the apparently horrendous weakening of the a1–h8 diagonal. Then White would have had two ways to attack: 18 h4 and 18 ♖de1. Later, during analysis which stretched over more than a year, it was established that Black can find a defence in either case. On 18 h4, he continues 18 ... ♘c5 19 h5 ♘xd3+ 20 ♖xd3 ♗f5 21 hg fg! 22 ♖xh7 ♔xh7 23 ♖e3 ♕c7 24 ♕e2 ♖a7! 25 ♗xa7 ♗d8.

And 18 ♖de1 ♗d8 19 ♕h3 is parried with 19 ... ♘e5 (Black loses after 19 ... ♗b6, because of 20 ♗xg6! fg 21 ♖e7) 20 ♕h6 ♗b6!, and after 21 fe ♗xd4 22 ♖e4 ♗f2 23 e6 the position is very unclear.

17 ... f5

Now White's dark-squared bishop becomes even stronger.

18 ♖de1 ♖f7

On 18 ... ♗d8, possible was a very interesting variation quoted by Tal: 19 ♕h5 ♘c5 20 ♗xg7! ♘xd3+ 21 ♔b1 (but not 21 cd? ♕c7+) 21 ... ♘xe1 22 g6 ♔xg7 23 ♕xh7+ ♔f6 24 g7 ♖f7 25 g8(♘) mate!

19 h4 ♗b7 *(133)*

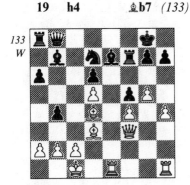

20 ♗xf5

Apparently stronger still was 20 g6 hg 21 h5 g5 22 ♗xf5, and then not 22 ... ♖xf5 23 ♖xe7 ♘e5, because of 24 h6! ♘xf3 25 h7+ ♔f8 26 ♖xg7 with inevitable mate.

20 ... ♖xf5
21 ♖xe7 ♘e5

The continuation 21 ... ♖f7 leads to a rout: 22 ♖xf7 ♔xf7 23 g6+ hg 24 h5.

22 ♕e4 ♕f8
23 fe ♖f4

After 23 ... ♖f1+ 24 ♖xf1 ♕xf1+ 25 ♔d2 Black does not have a single check.

24 ♕e3 ♖f3

The main variation of the combination begun with the move

20 ♗xf5 was 24 ... ♗xd5 25 ed ♖xd4 (25 ... ♗xh1 26 ♖xg7+ and Black's isolated pieces are helpless) 26 ♕xd4 ♗xh1 27 b3. It would probably be best for Black to return the piece immediately: 27 ... ♗f3 28 ♕c4+ ♚h8 29 ♖f7 ♕xd6 30 ♖xf3 a5, retaining some drawing chances.

	25	♕e2	♕xe7

Black gains nothing after 25 ... ♕f4+ 26 ♕d2 ♖f1+ 27 ♖xf1 ♕xf1+ 28 ♕d1, or 25 ... ♗xd5 26 ed.

	26	♕xf3	de
	27	♖e1	♖d8

The endgame after 27 ... ♖f8 28 ♖xe5 ♕xe5 29 ♕xf8+ ♚xf8 30 ♗xe5 would have guaranteed White an easy win — Black cannot capture on d5 because of 31 ♗d6+.

	28	♖xe5	♕d6
	29	♕f4!	

Now Black cannot play 29 ... ♗xd5, because of 30 ♖e8+!.

	29	...	♖f8
	30	♕e4	b3

Black is trying to get at least some chances.

	31	ab	♖f1+
	32	♚d2	♕b4+
	33	c3	

Now it is all over.

	33	...	♕d6
	34	♗c5!	

An elegant tactical trick: the black queen is deflected away from the e6-square.

	34	...	♕xc5
	35	♖e8+	♖f8
	35	♕e6+	♚h8
	37	♕f7	Black resigned.

Game No. 45
Ljubojevic–Tal
Las Palmas 1975

1	e4	c5
2	♘f3	e6
3	d4	cd
4	♘xd4	♘f6
5	♘c3	d6

6 g4

The celebrated Keres Attack, which for many years has been a source of headaches for those who play the Scheveningen Variation as Black.

6 ... a6
7 g5

White of course is not obliged to play this move, because also in the spirit of the 'extended fianchetto' (g2–g4!) is 7 ♗g2, which, however, would subsequently amount to transposition to the same schemes.

7 ... ♘fd7
8 h4

White was faced with a problem: should he allow ... b7–b5? The possible continuation 8 a4 ♘c6 9 ♗e3 ♘de5 10 ♘b3 ♘a5 11 ♘xa5 ♛xa5 12 f4 ♘c6 13 ♗g2 h6 leads to extremely complicated play, where the defect of White's position is the not entirely secure situation of his king, whether in the centre of the board or on either flank.

8 ... b5
9 h5 b4

The infantries of both armies have been thrown impetuously forward, leaving their commanding officers way behind. Worth considering was a preliminary 9 ... ♗b7!.

10 ♘ce2 ♗b7
11 ♗g2 ♘c5
12 ♘g3 ♘bd7

Attacking the e4-square further with 12 ... d5 would have led after 13 g6! de 14 gf+ ♔xf7 to an extremely double-edged situation. But all the same this would have been a consistent plan, whereas the text move is rather passive.

13 f4 ♗e7
14 ♛g4 h6
15 g6 *(134)*

One can imagine, writes Kirillov, the regret with which Lju-bojevic rejected the tempting 15 gh, with the following possible variation: 15 ... ♘f6 16 ♛xg7 ♜g8 17 ♛xg8+! ♘xg8 18 h7 and a new queen is born. But Black could have replied simply 15 ... gh, when White has achieved nothing.

15 ... 0–0
16 gf+

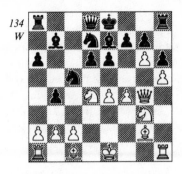

This exchange should not be postponed, in view of the counter-threat of 16 ... f5!.

16	...	♖xf7
17	♗e3	

The natural 17 ♘xe6 leads after 17 ... ♘xe6 18 ♕xe6 ♗h4 19 ♕g4 ♗xg3+ 20 ♕xg3 ♘f6! to a position where Black has the initiative.

17	...	♕c7
18	0–0!	

This looks surprising, but for the time being White is sufficiently strong on the kingside for his king to feel safe there. In the event of the standard 18 0–0–0 Black could have obtained good counterplay with 18 ... ♖c8 or 18 ... ♘f6 19 ♕g6 ♘cd7 (with 20 ... ♘f8 in mind) 20 ♘xe6 ♕c4 21 ♘f5 ♕xe6 22 ♘xh6+ ♔f8 23 ♗h3 ♕xa2!.

18	...	♗f6

Now 18 ... ♘f6? is not playable, in view of 19 ♕g6 ♘cd7 20 ♘xe6 ♕c4 21 ♘f5! ♕xe6 22 ♘xh6+ ♔f8 23 f5 ♘e5 (in this variation the pawn on a2 is defended!) 24 fe ♘xg6 25 hg when the ill-fated rook on f7 is attacked three times and does not have a single retreat-square.

19	♘xe6	♘xe6
20	♕xe6	♗xb2
21	♖ad1	

Stronger was 21 ♖ab1 followed by 22 ♘f5.

21	...	♘f6

Black has taken advantage of his breathing-space in order to transfer his knight to the kingside.

22	♕xd6	♘g4

23	♗b6	♕xc2
24	♕e6	

Having sensed that his advantage is slipping away, White begins to look for a way to develop his initiative into something more decisive. He would achieve nothing with 24 ♕xb4 ♖xf4! 25 ♖d2 ♕c3 26 ♕xc3 ♖xf1+, when chances are equal. Possibly stronger was 24 ♖d2 ♕c3 25 ♘e2 ♕f6 26 ♕xf6 ♖xf6 (26 ... ♗xf6 27 e5!) 27 ♗a5! when Black has definite problems.

24	...	♘f6
25	♘f5	

25 ♕b3 would scarcely achieve anything, because of 25 ... ♖c8!.

25	...	♖e8
26	♖d8	

Or 26 ♘e7+ ♖xe7 27 ♖d8+ ♖e8 28 ♖xe8+ ♘xe8 29 ♕xe8+ and White regains the piece, but no more than that.

26	...	♖xd8
27	♗xd8	♗xe4

Black would lose after 27 ... ♘xe4, because of 28 ♕e8+ ♖f8 29 ♘e7+.

28	♗xe4	♘xe4 *(135)*

The only move, since if Black captures with his queen there follows 29 ♕xf7+ and 30 ♘d6+.

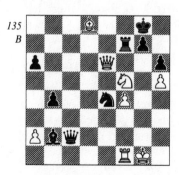

29	♗b6!	

Here White could not play 29 ♕e8+ ♖f8 30 ♘e7+ ♔h7 31 ♕xf8 because of 31 ... ♗d4+ and 32 ... ♘g3 mate.

29	...	♕d3!

The incursion of the black queen into the vicinity of the enemy king practically guarantees perpetual check.

30	♖e1 *(136)*	

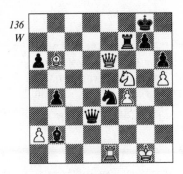

White achieves nothing with 30 &c5 &xc5 31 &e7+ &h7 32 ♕g6+ &h8!.

30	...	&d6!

The black knight is forced to retreat and even to offer itself up as a sacrifice, but in so doing it deflects the white knight away from the defence of the g3-square.

31	&xd6	♕g3+
32	&h1	

Nothing good would result from playing 32 &f1, because of 32 ... ♕xf4+.

32	...	♕f3+
33	&g1	Drawn.

9   Interference

With the aid of this tactical method either the connection between opposing pieces situated on the same line is broken or access to a key square is barred.

An interesting position arose after 44 moves of a telephone game between teams representing the towns of Maur-de-Fosses (France) and Essen (Germany) in 1986.

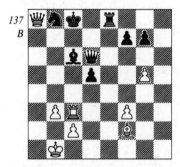

There now followed the diversionary tactic **1 ♗g3!** and the impression was that White was winning. After what would appear to be the only move, 1 ... ♛xg3, there follows 2 ♖xc6+ ♚d8 (but not 2 ... ♚d7 because of 3 ♛b7+ with mate) 3 ♛a5+ ♚d7! (Black loses at once after 3 ... ♚e7, as a result of 4 ♛b4+! and 5 ♛b7+) 4 ♛xd5+ ♚e7 5 ♛c5+ ♚d7 6 ♖b6 with irresistible threats.

Black replied with a move of rare beauty: **1 ... ♛c7!!**, with interference on the c-file, and obtained a winning position after 2 ♖xc6 ♛xc6 3 ♛xb8+ ♚d7 4 ♛a7+ ♚e6 5 ♛e3+ ♚f5.

Game No. 46
Karpov–Gik
Moscow 1968/69

1	e4	c5
2	♘f3	d6
3	d4	cd
4	♘xd4	♘f6
5	♘c3	g6

When this game was played the Dragon had, as it were, been reborn yet again. The history of this opening variation consists almost totally of 'ups and downs'. This game was a source of disappointment for adherents of the Dragon, and it is quite possible that it again (temporarily) buried one of its varieties.

6	♗e3	♗g7
7	f3	0–0
8	♗c4	♘c6
9	♕d2	♕a5

The most fashionable continuation at that time.

10	0–0–0	♗d7
11	h4	♘e5
12	♗b3	♖fc8

Another possible continuation is 12 ... ♖ac8, which also leads to a very complicated and double-edged game.

13	h5

White sacrifices a pawn, trying to get his forces mobilised as quickly as possible. Also encountered are the continuations 13 ♔b1 and 13 g4.

After the immediate 13 ♗h6 there may follow 13 ... ♗xh6 14 ♕xh6 ♖xc3!, when after 15 bc Black may choose either 15 ... ♕xc3 16 ♔b1 a5 17 a4 b5, or 15 ... ♕a3+ 16 ♔d2 a5 17 h5 g5! 18 ♕xg5+ ♔h8, after which White's attack comes to a dead-end (Gurvich–Dubinin, corr. 1968/69).

13	...	♘xh5
14	♗h6

Formerly this continuation was considered to be impossible, because of 14 ... ♘d3+, but then it became clear that also in this case White maintains an advantage after 15 ♔b1! ♘xb2 16 ♔xb2 ♗xh6 17 ♕xh6. White can also play 14 g4, since the sacrifice of a piece with 14 ... ♘xg4 15 fg ♗xg4 16 ♖df1 looks very risky. In the game Kauranen–Estrin, corr. 1968/70, after 14 ... ♘f6 15 ♖dg1 b5 16 ♗h6 ♖xc3! 17 ♕xc3 ♕xc3 18 bc Black obtained complete equality.

14	...	♗xh6

15	♕xh6	♖xc3
16	bc *(138)*	

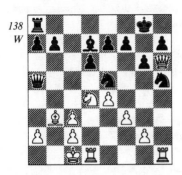

16	...	♕xc3?

As Karpov convincingly proves, this natural move is a decisive mistake. Worth considering was 16 ... ♘f6, and if White plays 17 g4 then it is indeed good to continue 17 ... ♕xc3! 18 ♘e2 ♕xf3.

In the game Smrcka–Estrin, corr. 1968/70, in reply to 16 ... ♘f6 White continued 17 ♔b1 b5 18 f4 ♘c4 19 e5 with double-edged play.

Also possible is 16 ... ♖c8, after which it is best for White to play 17 ♔b1 or 17 ♘e2.

17	♘e2!	

The start of a long forcing manoeuvre. The knight can cope excellently with the task of expelling the queen, and at the same time it comes to support the kingside attack.

17	...	♕c5

Stronger was 17 ... ♘d3+, when after 18 ♖xd3 ♕a1+ 19 ♔d2 ♕xh1 20 g4 ♘g3 21 ♕xh1 ♘xh1 22 ♔e3 h5 or 22 ... ♘g3 it is not easy for White to prove that he has compensation for the loss of two pawns.

18	g4	♘f6
19	g5	♘h5
20	♖xh5!	

A decisive exchange sacrifice. On 20 ♘g3 there would have followed 20 ... ♗g4! 21 fg ♘xg4 22 ♗xf7+ ♔h8!, when the white queen is trapped.

20	...	gh
21	♖h1	♕e3+
22	♔b1!	

As Karpov writes, the slightest inaccuracy can ruin a game. Thus, for example, 22 ♔b2 would have given Black at least a draw: 22 ... ♘d3+ 23 cd ♕xe2+ 24 ♔a1 ♕xd3 and Black has a perpetual at worst.

22	...	♕xf3

In the event of 22 ... ♕xe2 23 ♕xh5 e6 24 ♕xh7+ ♔f8 25 ♕h8+ ♔e7 26 ♕f6+ Black is mated.

23	♖xh5	e6 *(139)*

On 23 ... ♘g6 White could have continued either 24 ♖h1 (suggested by Zaitsev), followed by 25 ♘d4, or in accordance with analysis by Estrin: 24 ♕xh7+ ♔f8 25 ♕h6+! ♔e8 26 ♕h8+ ♘f8 27 ♖h7 e6 28 g6 fg 29 ♘d4 ♕xe4 30 ♕g8 ♕xd4 31 ♕f7+ ♔d8 32 ♕xf8+ ♔c7 33 ♕xa8, and the white king escapes from perpetual check (33 ... ♕d1+ 34 ♔b2 ♕d4+ 35 c3 ♕f2+ 36 ♗c2 ♕b6+ 37 ♔a1 ♕g1+ 38 ♗b1).

In the event of 23 ... ♕xe4 the game would have been concluded with 24 g6! (four times *en prise*!!) 24 ... ♕xg6 25 ♖g5.

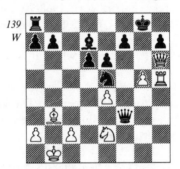

139
W

24	g6!	♘xg6

Other captures lose immediately: 24 ... hg 25 ♕h8 mate, or 24 ... fg 25 ♕xh7+ ♔f8 26 ♕h8+ ♔e7 27 ♖h7+ ♘f7 28 ♕xa8.

25	♕xh7+	♔f8 *(140)*
26	♖f5!!	

A very successful interference move on the f-file. Black does not have a single check and can only defend against mate by giving up his queen.

26	...	♕xb3+
27	ab	ef
28	♘f4!	

One more tactical trick. White exploits the undefended position

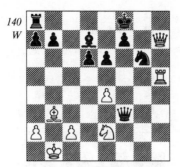

of the rook on a8 and deflects the knight from the defence of the
back rank.

28	...	♖d8
29	♕h6+	♚e8
30	♘xg6	fg
31	♕xg6+	♚e7
32	♕g5+!	

The hasty 32 ef would have allowed Black to hold out after 32
... ♖f8.

32	...	♚e8
33	ef	♖c8
34	♕g8+	♚e7
35	♕g7+	Black resigned.

Game No. 47
Karpov–Korchnoi
2nd game, Candidates Final, Moscow 1974

1	e4	c5
2	♘f3	d6
3	d4	cd
4	♘xd4	♘f6
5	♘c3	g6

Among the World's strongest players Korchnoi has been the
one to play the Dragon Variation most frequently.

6	♗e3	♗g7
7	f3	♘c6
8	♕d2	0–0
9	♗c4	♗d7
10	h4	♖c8

11	♗b3	♘e5
12	0–0–0	

Also possible is the immediate 12 h5.

12	...	♘c4
13	♗xc4	♖xc4
14	h5	♘xh5
15	g4	♘f6 *(141)*

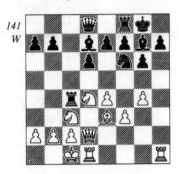

141
W

16	♘de2

This move was first suggested by E. Chumak, a player from Dnepropetrovsk. The basic idea of the move 16 ♘de2 is the consolidation of the c3-square. The point is that after a typical exchange-sacrifice (... ♖xc3), doubling White's pawns on the c-file, Black's position is so rich with possibilities that even without an attack, even in the endgame, he can maintain the equilibrium. In addition, the white knight can now easily be transferred from e2 for a direct attack on the enemy king.

16	...	♕a5

Stronger is 16 ... ♖e8 (see Game 51; Pouso–Nesis and Game 52; Eisen–Nesis).

17	♗h6	♗xh6

Playing 17 ... ♖fc8 18 ♗xg7 ♔xg7 19 ♕h6+ ♔g8 would amount to transposition.

18	♕xh6	♖fc8
19	♖d3!	

A novelty, which had been prepared for this match. It had been established that the continuation 19 ♖d5 offers White no real advantage in any line. For example: 19 ... ♕d8 20 g5 ♘h5 21 ♘g3 ♕f8! 22 ♕xf8+ ♖xf8! 23 ♘xh5 gh 24 ♖xh5 f5!, and here Black stands slightly better. Or 20 e5 de 21 g5 ♘h5 22 ♘g3 ♕f8

23 ♖xh5 (23 ♘xh5 ♕xh6 24 gh ♗c6!) 23 … gh 24 ♖xd7 ♕xh6 25 gh and Black's remote passed pawn on the h-file gives him good counter-chances.

The move 19 ♖d3! additionally strengthens the c3-square and therefore frees the knight on e2 for White's attack in a number of variations. If White had tried to go forward at once without this move, by playing 19 g5 ♘h5 20 ♘g3, an unpleasant counter-punch would have awaited him: 20 … ♖xc3; but now this need not be feared.

19 … ♖4c5 *(142)*

The best practical chance for Black was the retreat 19 … ♕d8, suggested by Botvinnik.

142
W

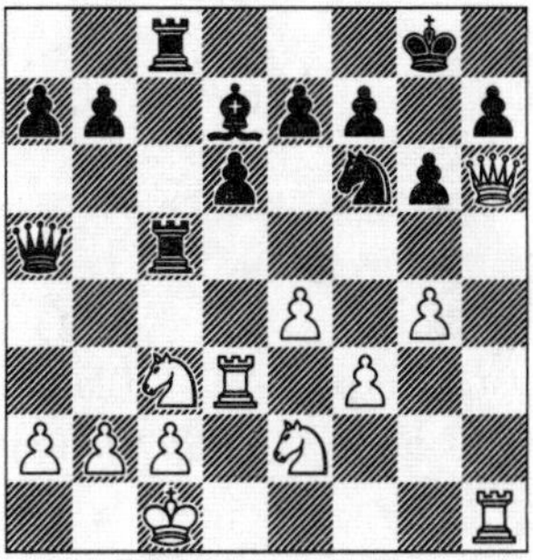

20 g5! ♖xg5

If 20 … ♘h5 then 21 ♘f4 would be very unpleasant.

21 ♖d5! ♖xd5

22 ♘xd5 ♖e8

But here it would not be good to play 22 … ♕d8, because of 23 ♘ef4 ♗c6 24 ♘xf6+ ef 25 ♕xh7+ ♔f8 26 ♘e6+ fe 27 ♕h8+ with mate.

23 ♘ef4 ♗c6 *(143)*

It is essential to take aim at the d5-square, otherwise White will play 24 ♘xf6+ and 25 ♘d5, with mate. On 23 … ♗e6 there would follow 24 ♘xe6 fe 25 ♘xf6+ ef 26 ♕xh7+ ♔f8 27 ♕xb7 ♕g5+ 28 ♔b1 ♖e7 29 ♕b8+ ♖e8 30 ♕xa7 (but not 30 ♖h8+?? ♔g7!, and it is Black who wins) 30 … ♖e7 31 ♕b8+ ♖e8 32 ♕xd6+.

Now it turns out that the direct 24 ♘xf6+ does not win: 24 … ef 25 ♘h5 ♕g5+! 26 ♕xg5 fg 27 ♘f6+ ♔g7 28 ♘xe8+ ♗xe8. But White finds an accurate route to victory.

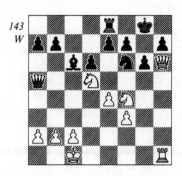

143
W

$$24 \quad e5!$$

Again an interference move on the fifth rank!

$$24 \quad \ldots \quad \text{♗xd5}$$

After 24 ... de 25 ♘xf6+ ef 26 ♘h5 mate is unavoidable.

25	ef	ef
26	♕xh7+	

Of course, not 26 ♘h5?? ♖e1+.

26	...	♚f8
27	♕h8+	Black resigned.

On 27 ... ♚e7, there follows 28 ♘xd5+ ♕xd5 29 ♖e1+.

Game No. 48
Kasparov–J. Piket
Tilburg 1989

1	e4	c5
2	♘f3	d6
3	d4	cd
4	♘xd4	♘f6
5	♘c3	g6
6	♗e3	♗g7
7	f3	♘c6
8	♕d2	0–0
9	♗c4	♗d7
10	h4	♘e5
11	♗b3	♖c8
12	0–0–0	♘c4
13	♗xc4	♖xc4
14	h5	♘xh5
15	g4	♘f6

16	♗h6	♘xe4

After 16 ... ♗xh6 17 ♕xh6 ♖xc3 18 g5! ♘h5 19 ♖xh5 gh 20 ♖h1 ♕c8 21 ♖xh5 ♗f5 22 ef ♖xc2+ 23 ♘xc2 ♕xf5 24 g6! White wins.

17	♕e3	♖xc3

But not 17 ... ♘xc3 18 ♗xg7 ♔xg7 19 ♕h6+ ♔f6 20 g5+ and White wins. White also wins after 17 ... ♘f6 18 ♗xg7 ♔xg7 19 ♕h6+ followed by 20 ♘d5.

18	bc	♘f6
19	♗xg7	♔xg7
20	♖h2	

A strong continuation, first played in the 4th game of the Candidates match Geller–Korchnoi, Moscow 1971.

White prepares for operations down the h-file, at the same time maintaining his pressure along the open central files. Previously in this position White had played 20 ♕h6+ ♔h8 21 ♖h2 ♖g8, and Black had succeeded in repelling the immediate threats to his king and in subsequent exploiting the irreparable weaknesses on White's queenside.

20	...	♖h8! *(144)*

On 20 ... ♖g8 unpleasant is 21 ♘e2!.

In the game Geller–Korchnoi mentioned above Black played 20 ... ♕a5, but after 21 ♘b3! ♕xa2 22 ♕xe7 ♕a3+ 23 ♔b1 ♖e8 24 ♕xd6 ♕xd6 25 ♖xd6 h6 26 ♘d4 White obtained a considerable advantage.

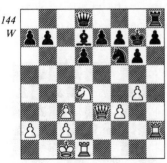

144
W

21	♘b3!

A significant improvement to this variation. White achieves nothing after 21 ♖dh1 h5 22 gh ♘xh5.

21	...	♗c6!

The best reply. White gets an undoubted advantage after 21 ...
♕b6 22 ♕h6+ ♔g8 23 ♖e2 e6 24 c4, or 21 ... b6 22 ♖e1! e5 23
♕h6+ ♔g8 24 ♖d2, and also 21 ... h5 22 g5! ♘h7 23 f4.

	22	g5!	♘h5
	23	f4	♖e8!

The active 23 ... ♕d7?! 24 ♘d4 ♕g4 25 ♕xe7 ♕xf4+ 26 ♔b2
♗d5 (not 26 ... ♕xh2 because of 27 ♘e6+, mating) 27 ♖e2 ♘g3
would lead after 28 ♖e3, with the threat of 29 ♖f3, to a difficult
position for Black.

	24	f5	♕b6
	25	♘d4	♕c5
	26	♖e1	♗d7!

This is stronger than 26 ... ♔g8 27 ♘xc6 ♕xe3+ (Black loses
after 27 ... ♕xc6? 28 fg hg 29 ♖xh5 gh 30 g6 d5 31 ♖g1! ♔g7
32 gf+ ♔xf7 33 ♕f3+ ♕f6 34 ♕xh5+ ♔f8 35 ♕h7) 28 ♖xe3 bc
29 c4! ♘g7 30 fg hg 31 ♖eh3 ♘h5 32 ♖a3 ♖a8 33 c5!.

	27	♕f3	♗c6
	28	♕e3	♗d7
	29	♕f3	♗c6
	30	♕f2?!	

Kasparov considers that a stronger continuation was 30 ♘xc6!
bc (or 30 ... ♕xc6 31 ♕e3) 31 ♖e3, when White has rather the
better prospects.

	30	...	♔g8?

Black wrongly rejects the obvious 30 ... ♕xc3. In this case after
31 ♖xe7 ♖xe7 32 f6+ ♔f8 33 fe+ ♔e8 34 ♘xc6 bc the game
would most probably have ended in a draw.

	31	♖e3	♗d5 *(145)*

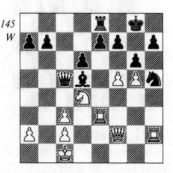

	32	♖xh5!	

The only way for White to convert his advantage into victory.

| 32 | ... | gh |
| 33 | ♕h4 | ♕c4 |

Even the relatively best 33 ... ♔h8 would not have saved Black, in view of the following variation: 34 ♕xh5 ♖g8 35 ♖h3 ♖g7 36 f6 ef 37 gf ♖g1+ 38 ♔b2 ♗e4 39 ♕xf7 ♕e5 40 ♖h5 ♕f4 41 ♕e8+ ♖g8 42 f7.

34	♕xh5	♕f1+
35	♔b2	e5
36	♕h6!	♔h8
37	g6	fg
38	fg	♖e7 *(146)*

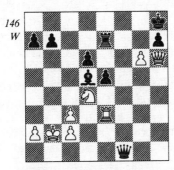

| 39 | ♖f3! |

A spectacular conclusion, involving the idea of interference.

| 39 | ... | ♕c4 |
| 40 | ♕f8+ | Black resigned. |

Game No. 49
Brunner–Hübner
W. Germany 1989

1	e4	c5
2	♘f3	d6
3	d4	cd
4	♘xd4	♘f6
5	♘c3	♘c6
6	♗c4	e6
7	♗e3	♗e7
8	♕e2	a6
9	0–0–0	♕c7

10	♗b3	0–0
11	♖hg1	

In Game 12 (Szmetan–G. Garcia) and Game 37 (Wahls–Hübner), White played 11 g4 immediately.

11	...	♘d7

An alternative to this continuation is 11 ... b5 12 g4, and now Black has three possibilities.

(a) 12 ... ♘xd4 13 ♗xd4 ♘d7 14 g5 ♘c5 (but not 14 ... b4 15 ♘d5! ed 16 ♗xd5 ♗b7 17 g6! hg 18 ♖xg6 ♘e5 19 ♖xg7+ ♔xg7 20 ♕g4+) 15 ♕h5 ♗b7 16 ♖g3 ♖fc8 17 f3 ♘xb3+ 18 ab a5 19 ♖h3 h6 20 ♖g1! with an irresistible attack for White (Valenti–Toth, Reggio Emilia 1975/76);

(b) 12 ... ♘a5 13 g5 ♘xb3+ 14 ab ♘d7 15 f4 b4 16 ♘f5! ♘c5 17 ♘xe7+ ♕xe7 18 e5!? bc 19 ed cb+ 20 ♔xb2 ♘a4+ 21 ba ♕b7+ 22 ♔c1 ♖b8 with unclear play (*ECO*);

(c) 12 ... b4 13 ♘xc6 ♕xc6 14 ♘d5! ed 15 g5 ♘xe4 16 ♗xd5 ♕a4 17 ♗xe4 (on 17 ♗xa8 there follows 17 ... ♘c3 18 bc ♗e6, with a difficult position for White) 17 ... ♗e6 18 ♗d4 g6 19 f4 with an unclear position (*ECO*).

12	g4

12 ♕h5 was considered in Game 42; Ivanovic–Larsen.

12	...	♘c5 *(147)*

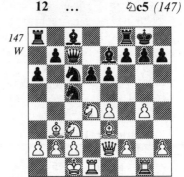

147
W

13	♔b1

This was the first time that this move had been played. The theoretical continuation is 13 g5 (13 f4 b5 14 f5 ♖e8 15 g5 g6!), in order on 13 ... ♗d7 to play 14 ♕h5 ♖fc8 15 ♖g3. But Black maintains the equilibrium: 15 ... g6 16 ♕h6 ♗f8 17 ♕h4 ♘xb3+ 18 ab ♗e7!, with 19 ... h5! in mind. Worth considering is 13 ♘f5!? b5 (13 ... ♘xb3+ 14 ab ef 15 ♘d5 ♕d8 16 gf leads to a very strong attack for White) 14 ♗d5!?, but all the same after 14 ... ed! 15 ♘xd5 ♕b7 16 e5 ♘e6 17 ed ♗d8 18 g5 ♔h8 Black's defence holds (Koops–Skrodelis, corr. 1986).

The continuation 13 ♔b1 sets Black complex problems regarding his choice of move. The tempting 13 ... b5?! is refuted by the continuation 14 ♘xc6! ♕xc6 15 ♘d5, and now 15 ... ♗d8 16 g5! ♘xb3 17 ♘f6+ ♔h8 (17 ... gf? 18 gf+ ♔h8 19 ♕g4 ♗xf6 20 ♗h6! is bad for Black) 18 ♕h5 gf 19 ♕h6 ♖g8 20 gf ♕e8 21 ♖g7, or 15 ... ♕b7 16 g5! ♘xb3 (if 16 ... ed then 17 ♗xd5 ♕b8 18 g6! hg 19 ♖xg6, with the threat 20 ♖xg7+!) 17 ♘f6+! ♔h8 18 ♕h5 gf 19 gf ♗xf6 20 ♗h6! ♕e7 21 ♕g4 leads to a win for White.

| 13 | ... | ♖e8?! |

It looks preferable to play 13 ... ♗d7 14 g5 b5, when Black has a very promising attack.

14	g5	♗d7
15	f4!?	b5
16	f5	♘xb3
17	ab	b4? *(148)*

The first impression is that Black has seized the initiative, as the knight on c3 has no good retreat-squares. But his opponent's 'bayonet thrust' came as a complete surprise — otherwise Black would have played 17 ... g6!, suppressing White's attack to a considerable extent.

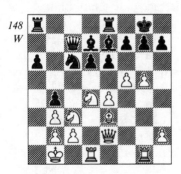

148
W

18 g6!

It now turns out that the white knight on c3 cannot be captured. If 18 ... bc then 19 gf+ ♔xf7 20 fe+ ♗xe6 21 ♕h5+ is decisive.

| 18 | ... | fg |
| 19 | fg | hg |

Better was 19 ... h6, when the black king is relatively safe.

| 20 | ⬛xg6 | ♗f8 |
| 21 | ⬛dg1! | |

The white knight is still invulnerable: 21 ... bc 22 ♕h5 ♘e5 23 ⬛h6 (with the threat 24 ⬛h8 mate) 23 ... ♘f7 24 ⬛h7 ⬛e7 25 ♗h6!! ♔xh7 (or 25 ... ♘e5 26 ⬛h8+!!) 26 ♗xg7+ ♔g8 27 ♗f6+ ♘g5! 28 ♕xg5+ ♗g7 29 ♗xg7.

21	...	♘e5
22	⬛h6	♘f7
23	⬛h3	♕a5 *(149)*

The threat was 24 ♕h5.

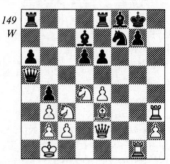

149
W

| 24 | ♘f5! | |

For the sake of invading with his queen White sacrifices his knight, with interference on the fifth rank.

24	...	ef
25	♕h5	♘e5
26	♘d5!	

For eight moves White's queen's knight was *en prise*, but finally it makes a decisive leap. The threat is 27 ♘f6+.

26	...	⬛e6
27	♕h7+	♔f7
28	⬛hg3!	

Now Black is defenceless.

28	...	♔e8
29	⬛xg7	♗xg7
30	⬛xg7	♔d8
31	♗b6+	♕xb6
32	♘xb6	⬛a7
33	ef	Black resigned.

Game No. 50
Gufeld–Espig
Leipzig 1980

1	e4	c5
2	♘f3	e6
3	d4	cd
4	♘xd4	♘f6
5	♘c3	d6
6	f4	a6
7	♗d3!?	♛c7
8	0–0	b5
9	a3	

White also gets no advantage after 9 a4 b4 10 ♘a2 ♗b7 11 ♛e2 ♘bd7.

9	...	♗b7
10	♛e2	♘bd7
11	♔h1	♗e7
12	♗d2	♖c8
13	b4!?	

The usual continuation in this position is 13 ♖ae1, but White wanted to try out a new plan.

| 13 | ... | ♘b6!? |
| 14 | a4 | |

Worth considering was 14 e5.

| 14 | ... | ba |
| 15 | b5!? | |

White obtains nothing from the variation 15 ♗xa6 ♗xa6 16 ♛xa6 0–0 17 ♛d3 ♘c4.

| 15 | ... | ab |

Worse was 15 ... d5, because of 16 ♘c6!.

| 16 | ♘cxb5 | |

This capture offers better prospects than 16 ♘dxb5, after which Black would play his trumps: 16 ... ♛b8 17 ♘xa4 ♘xa4 18 ♖xa4 0–0 19 ♗b4 ♗c6!. Nevertheless it is clear that White should have continued 16 ♗xb5+ ♘fd7 17 f5 e5 18 ♘e6!? fe 19 fe ♗c6 20 ♗xc6, when after 20 ... ♛xc6 21 ed+ ♛xd7 22 ♛f2! he would have had the better chances.

| 16 | ... | ♛b8 |
| 17 | ♗b4 | |

This looks stronger than 17 e5 de 18 fe ♘fd7 19 ♖ae1 ♘c5.

17	...	♘fd7!

Preventing White from playing e4–e5.

18	♖ae1	♘c5
19	e5	

White achieves nothing with 19 ♘f5, in view of the simple 19 ... ef 20 ef 0–0 21 ♕xe7 ♘xd3.

19	...	de
20	fe	0–0 (150)

Considerably weaker was 20 ... ♘xd3, in view of 21 ♘d6+.

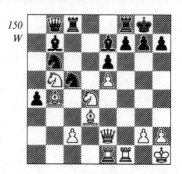

150
W

White should not delay any further, and he now proceeded to take decisive action.

21	♗xh7!?

A different attack also deserved consideration: 21 ♗xc5, which would have been justified in the event of 21 ... ♖xc5? 22 ♘xe6! fe 23 ♕h5 ♖f5 24 ♖xf5 ef 25 ♕xf5 g6 26 ♕e6+. Playing 24 ... g6 25 ♖g5 ♗xg5 26 ♕xg5 would also not help Black.

But after 21 ... ♗xc5 the best White can reckon on is a draw: 22 ♘xe6 fe 23 ♕h5 ♖f5! 24 ♖xf5 ef 25 ♕xf5 g6 26 ♕e6+ ♔h8, since 27 ♘d6 gets White nowhere because of 27 ... ♖f8!.

It is not correct to play 22 ♗xh7+? ♔xh7 23 ♕h5+ ♔g8 24 ♖e3, in view of 24 ... ♕a8! 25 ♖f2 ♕a5 26 c3 ♕xb5!.

21	...	♔xh7
22	♕h5+	♔g8
23	♖e3	♕a8

Also possible was 23 ... f6, when after 24 ♕g4 interesting complications could have arisen.

24	♖g3	♗e4 (151)
25	♖f5!!	

This is the only way to accomplish the idea of interference! As

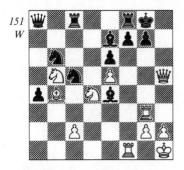

151
W

for 25 ♘f5?!, this move can be spectacularly refuted: 25 ... ef 26 ♕h6 ♘e6 27 ♗xe7 ♖xc2 28 ♗f6 ♖xg2!.

25	...	♗xf5
26	♘xf5	ef
27	♘d6! *(152)*	

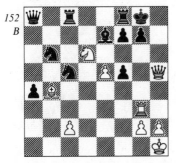

152
B

It turns out that after 27 ... ♘e6 28 ♘xf5 ♗xb4 29 ♖xg7+! ♘xg7 30 ♕g5 Black is mated. Therefore he is forced to release the tension.

27	...	♗xd6!
28	♖xg7+	♔xg7

Drawn by perpetual check.

10 The Pin

All tactical tricks involving a pin are based on the exploitation of the total or partial lack of mobility of enemy pieces.

Trapl–Prandstetter
Ostrava 1976

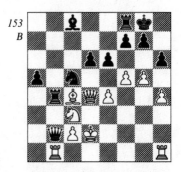

153
B

A typical Sicilian position. White has a menacing attack on the kingside, but Black's counter-offensive is coming to a dead-end: after 1 ... ♕a3 2 gh, or 1 ... e5 2 ♕e3 it will not be easy for him to create counterplay. An unexpected tactical trick comes to the rescue.

| 1 | ... | ♘b3+!! |

It turns out that the knight cannot be captured.

2	♔d3	♘xd4
3	♖xb2	♖xb2
4	♔xd4	♖xc2

And Black won.

Game No. 51
Pouso–Nesis
World Corr. Ch. 1980/82

1	e4	c5
2	♘f3	d6
3	d4	cd
4	♘xd4	♘f6
5	♘c3	g6
6	♗e3	♗g7
7	f3	♘c6
8	♕d2	0-0
9	♗c4	♗d7
10	0-0-0	♖c8
11	♗b3	♘e5
12	h4	♘c4
13	♗xc4	♖xc4
14	h5	♘xh5
15	g4	♘f6
16	♘de2	♖e8

This move is an improvement to Black's play in this position, which was first encountered in the 2nd game of the Candidates Final, Karpov–Korchnoi, Moscow 1974 (see Game 47).

| 17 | ♗h6 | ♗h8! |

This looks like an oversight, but Black's resources are very considerable.

| 18 | e5 *(154)* |

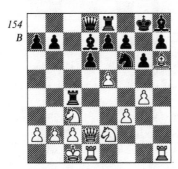

154
B

Now on 18 ... de White plays 19 g5.

| 18 | ... | ♘xg4! |
| 19 | fg | ♗xe5 |

It would be worse for Black to play 19 ... ♗xg4, in view of 20 ed ♕xd6 21 ♕xd6 ed 22 ♖xd6, and the knight on e2 cannot be captured because of the weakness of Black's back rank.

20	♗f4	♛a5
21	♗xe5	♛xe5

White has succeeded in exchanging dark-squared bishops, but in the process the black queen has occupied an excellent position in the centre of the board, taking control of several key squares.

22	g5	b5
23	♘d4	b4
24	♘ce2	♖ec8
25	♔b1	♗g4!	*(155)*

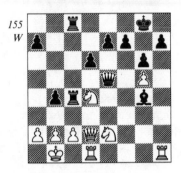

155
W

An unpleasant pin. The white knights are essentially not playing any part in the game.

26	♖c1	♗xe2
27	♘xe2	♖8c5!
28	♖hg1	♖d5
29	♛e1	♖e4

Note the complete dominance of the black pieces!

30	♖g2	♛e6

With the threat of 31 ... ♖de5.

31	♛f1	♖d2

White resigned.

After 32 ♘g3 ♖xg2 33 ♛xg2 ♖e1 White has no chance to save the game.

Game No. 52
Eisen–Nesis
corr. match USA–USSR 1980/82

1	e4	c5
2	♘f3	d6

3	d4	cd
4	♘xd4	♘f6
5	♘c3	g6
6	♗e3	♗g7
7	f3	♘c6
8	♕d2	0–0
9	♗c4	♗d7
10	0–0–0	♖c8
11	♗b3	♘e5
12	h4	♘c4
13	♗xc4	♖xc4
14	h5	

Sometimes White plays 14 g4, which is certainly no worse than the traditional 14 h5.

14	...	♘xh5
15	g4	♘f6
16	♘de2	♖e8
17	♗h6	♗h8
18	e5	♘xg4
19	fg	♗xe5
20	♗f4	

Play becomes complicated after 20 ♘d5!?. In the game Kutyanin–Nesis, corr. 1977/78, there followed: 20 ... ♗xg4 21 ♘e3 ♖a4 22 ♘xg4 ♖xg4 23 ♖df1 ♕b6 24 c3 ♕c6 25 ♗e3 h5 26 ♖hg1 ♖xg1 27 ♖xg1 a6 28 ♕d3 ♗g7.

20	...	♕a5
21	♗xe5	♕xe5 *(156)*

I had already encountered all these moves in other games of mine. In the 13th USSR Correspondence Championship 1977/78, Zborovsky played 22 ♕h6 against me, but he was subsequently forced to fight for a draw. In the final of the 2nd ICCF Cup Lecroq played 22 ♘d5, and the game ended in defeat for the French Master. Neither did the American player's idea turn out to be justified. White's threats on the kingside turned out to be rather ineffectual, whereas Black's offensive on the other wing quickly achieved its aim.

22	g5	b5
23	♘d4	b4
24	♘ce2	♖ec8
25	♖h4	

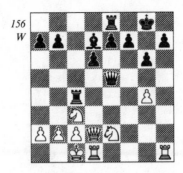

25 ⊈b1 is not much better, as we saw in the previous game, Pouso-Nesis.

| | 25 | ... | ⊈a4! |
| | 26 | b3 *(157)* | |

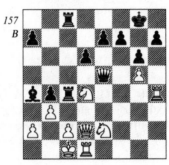

| | 26 | ... | ⧄xc2+! |

It turns out that after 27 ⧄xc2 there follows 27 ... ♛a1 mate — the pin of the knight on c2 works quite well!

27	♛xc2	♛xg5+
28	⧄f4	⧄xc2+
29	⊈xc2	

The disparity in the forces remaining on the board is quite improbable: Black has a queen and five (!) pawns for two rooks and a minor piece. Unfortunately for White he has no counter-chances at all.

29	...	e5
30	⧄ff1	⊈d7
31	⧄f3	⊈f5+
32	⊈b2	♛g2
33	⧄de1	⊈d3

34	♘h4	♛e4

White resigned.

Game No. 53
Yudasin–Aseev
Leningrad 1989

1	e4	c5
2	♘f3	d6
3	d4	cd
4	♘xd4	♘f6
5	♘c3	♘c6
6	♗g5	e6
7	♛d2	♗e7
8	0–0–0	0–0
9	♘b3	a6
10	♗xf6	gf
11	f4	

A common continuation is 11 ♛h6. Now after 11 ... ♔h8 12 ♛h5 ♛e8 13 f4 ♖g8 14 g4 b5 15 ♗d3 ♖g7 16 h4 b4 17 ♘e2 a complicated position arises, in which Black has quite good prospects. For example, 17 ... a5 18 g5 a4 19 ♘bd4 b3 (but not 19 ... ♘xd4 20 ♘xd4 ♗d7 21 gf ♗xf6 22 e5 de 23 ♖hg1 ♛g8 Arnason–Inkiov, Plovdiv 1986 and now White should have played 24 ♘f3!) 20 ab ab 21 ♘xb3 ♗b7 22 ♘c3 ♘b4 23 ♖hg1 ♛c6! 24 ♖g3 ♛b6 25 ♛e2 d5 with the initiative for the sacrificed pawn (Psakhis–Kotronias, Dortmund 1989).

Black also gets good chances with 17 ... e5 18 f5 a5 19 ♔b1 a4 20 ♘bc1 ♗b7 21 ♖hg1 ♘b8 22 g5 ♘d7 (Oll–Aseev, Odessa 1989).

| 11 | ... | ♔h8 |

Worth considering is the more energetic 11 ... b5.

| 12 | f5 | b5 |

After 12 ... ef 13 ♗d3 fe 14 ♘xe4 f5 15 ♛c3+ ♘e5 16 ♘g3 White has a marked advantage.

| 13 | ♘e2 *(158)* | |
| 13 | ... | ♖e8!? |

An unclear position would arise after 13 ... ef!? 14 ef (14 ♛d5 ♘b4 15 ♛xa8 ♛c7 16 ♘bd4 ♗d7 17 ♛xf8+ ♗xf8 favours Black) 14 ... ♘e5!? 15 ♘bd4 ♗b7; worse for Black is 13 ... ♗d7? 14 ♘f4 (with the threat 15 fe fe 16 ♘g6+! hg 17 ♛h6+) 14 ... ♖g8 15 fe fe 16 ♘c5 dc 17 ♛xd7 with the advantage.

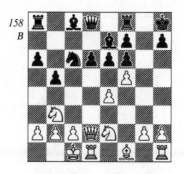

14	♕h6	♖g8
15	g3	♖g5
16	♘f4	♗f8
17	♕h4	♕e7

As a result of Black's accurate manoeuvring White's initiative on the kingside has run out of steam, and the white queen has ended up in a rather awkward position.

18	♔b1	♗d7
19	♗e2	♖e8
20	♖hf1	ef
21	ef	♗xf5
22	♗d3	♗xd3
23	♖xd3	♕e4

More accurate was 23 ... ♕d8.

24	a3	♘e5
25	♘d2	♕a8
26	♖d4	♘g6
27	♕h3	♘xf4
28	♖dxf4	♖g6!

It turns out that 29 ♖xf6 ♖xf6 30 ♖xf6 ♖e1+ 31 ♔a2 ♕d5+ 32 ♘b3 ♕d1 32 ♘a5 ♕xc2 leads to a win for Black.

29	♘f3	♖e2
30	♖h4	h6
31	♕f5	

The manoeuvre 31 ♘d4 and 32 ♘f5 would have set Black greater problems.

31	...	♕e8
32	♘d4	♖e1+
33	♖xe1	♕xe1+

34	♔a2	♛e8
35	♖e4	♛a8
36	♖e2	♝g7?!

By no means the best move, but it provoked a tactical error from White.

37 ♘e6?? *(159)*

White would have stood clearly better after 37 ♖e7 ♖g5 38 ♛d7 ♛d5+ 39 ♘b3.

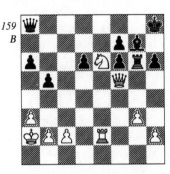

159
B

37	...	♛c8!

This move combines a pin with the threat of a double attack.

38 ♘xg7

It would not help to play 38 b3, in view of 38 ... ♖g5! (here the pin is really telling!), and 38 ♘d4 was bad because of 38 ... ♛c4+.

38	...	♛c4+
39	♔b1	♛xe2
40	♘h5	♛e1+

White resigned.

Game No. 54
Khalifman–Kasparov
USSR Ch., Moscow 1988

1	e4	c5
2	♘f3	e6
3	d4	cd
4	♘xd4	♘f6
5	♘c3	d6
6	♝e3	a6
7	♛d2	♝e7

	8	**f3**	♞c6
	9	**0–0–0**	

This move is not the most accurate, since with 9 ... d5 Black can transpose into a roughly equal ending after 10 ed ♞xd5 11 ♞xd5 ♛xd5 12 ♞b3 ♛xd2+ 13 ♜xd2 ♝d7. It is more precise to play 9 g4.

	9	**...**	0–0
	10	**g4**	♜b8

Grandmaster Suba's idea. The game Short–Kasparov, Belfort 1988, continued: 10 ... ♞d7 11 h4 ♞de5 12 ♞xc6 bc 13 ♝e2 ♜b8 14 g5 d5 15 ♝a7 ♜b7 16 ♝d4 ♞d7 17 ed cd 18 f4 ♛a5 19 ♛e3 ♞b8! and Black eventually won.

But White should have played 15 ♝d4 at once, after which the black knight would not have had the square b8.

	11	**h4**	♞xd4
	12	**♝xd4**	♞d7
	13	**g5**	

It is not good to play 13 ♝d3, in view of 13 ... b5 14 g5 b4 15 ♞e2 ♞e5.

	13	**...**	b5
	14	**♚b1**	♛c7

Black removes his queen from the d-file in order to ensure that his knight can jump to e5 or c5.

	15	**h5**	b4
	16	**♞e2**	

In the event of 16 ♞a4 Black does not play 16 ... ♞e5 (because of 17 ♛f2 ♝d7 18 ♞b6 when play is unclear) but 16 ... ♞c5! 17 ♞xc5 dc, since 18 ♝f6 gf 19 gf ♝xf6 20 ♜g1+ ♚h8 21 ♛h6 ♛e7 does not give White compensation; for example: 22 ♝xa6!? ♝xa6 23 ♜d7 ♜g8!.

	16	**...**	♞e5 *(160)*
	17	**♞g1!**	

A paradoxical move, but the only one that prevents Black from developing an initiative. In the event of 17 f4 Black would have obtained a good position: 17 ... ♞c4 18 ♛d3 e5 19 ♞c1 ♝e6.

	17	**...**	f5!

A sharp and timely reply. Inferior was 17 ... ♞c4 18 ♝xc4 ♛xc4 19 b3 ♛c6, when White has a pleasant choice between 20 h6 and 20 g6.

	18	**gf**	♝xf6

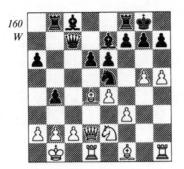

| 19 | h6 | g6 |
| 20 | b3! | &b7 |

More accurate was 20 ... ♛e7!.

| 21 | &h3 | ♛e7 |
| 22 | ♖h2?! | |

Worth considering was 22 &b2!, attacking two black pawns, and now after 22 ... ♘xf3 23 ♘xf3 &xb2 24 ♔xb2 ♖xf3 25 ♛xb4 White would have had a clear advantage.

| 22 | ... | a5! |

The roles have changed. Black has defended his weaknesses and is now ready to attack the white king.

23	♖e2	♘f7
24	&xf6	♛xf6
25	f4	♖bc8?!

Black had a stronger continuation: 25 ... e5! 26 f5 ♘g5!, seizing the initiative.

| 26 | ♘f3! | |

It turns out that in the event of 26 ... ♖c3 27 ♘g5 ♘xg5 28 fg ♛e5 White has the quiet move 29 &g2!.

26	...	♛c3
27	♖e3	♛xd2
28	♖xd2?	*(161)*

But this is undoubtedly a mistake. After 28 ♘xd2!, followed by 29 ♘c4, Black would have had serious problems.

| 28 | ... | ♖c3! |

Now White is forced to go for complications. It would be bad to play 29 ♖dd3 now because of 29 ... ♖xd3 30 cd ♘xh6, when White cannot save his pawn on f4.

| 29 | ♖xc3 | bc |

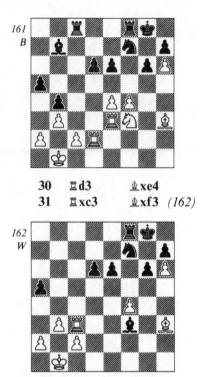

30	🜚d3	♝xe4
31	🜚xc3	♝xf3 *(162)*

It would appear that everything is quite clear: after the natural 32 🜚xf3 ♞g5 33 🜚e3 ♞xh3 34 🜚xh3 🜚xf4 Black has a winning ending, but by making use of a pin White finds a spectacular way to save the game.

32	♝xe6!	♝h5

Black also achieves nothing with 32 ... ♝e2 33 🜚c7 ♝b5 34 a4 ♝e8, in view of 35 b4!.

33	🜚c7	g5
34	fg	🜚e8

A draw was now agreed, since after 35 ♝f5 Black has nothing better than 35 ... ♝g6 36 ♝xg6 hg 37 ♔b2 ♞xg5 38 🜚g7+ ♔h8 39 🜚xg6 ♞e4 40 🜚g7.

11 The Back Rank

Tactical operations which exploit the weakness of the back rank by threatening mate are extremely common in chess practice.

An excellent example is the conclusion of the game Vikman–Kanko, Finland 1975.

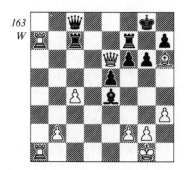

After an exchange of queens White would have considerable difficulties in turning his advantage into victory; but it turns out that the exchange of queens can be avoided.

1   ♖d1!!

The white queen cannot be taken, because of mate on the back rank (2 ♖d8+). White also threatens 2 ♖xc7 ♕xc7 3 ♕e8+; but the main variation is 1 ... ♗c6 2 ♖xc7! ♕xe6 (after 2 ... ♕xc7 White plays 3 ♕xc6) 3 ♖xc6 ♕e8 4 ♖cd6, when there is no defence against 5 ♖d8. 1 ... ♗b7 does not help, because of 2 ♖xb7! ♕xe6 3 ♖d8+.

Black resigned.

Game No. 55
Kokkonen–Nesis
European Corr. Ch. 1978/79
1   e4   c5

2	♘f3	d6
3	d4	cd
4	♘xd4	♘f6
5	♘c3	g6
6	♗e3	♗g7
7	f3	0–0
8	♕d2	♘c6
9	♗c4	♗d7
10	h4	♖c8
11	♗b3	♘e5
12	0–0–0	♘c4
13	♗xc4	♖xc4
14	g4	

The drawback of this plan is White's delay in organising a pawn storm.

14	...	b5!

14 ... ♕c7 is also playable, see Game 27; Ivanchuk–A. Schneider.

15	h5	

The move 15 ♘dxb5 (15 ♘cxb5 is not playable, because of 15 ... e5) leads after 15 ... ♕a5 16 ♘d4 ♖fc8 to a position where Black has excellent attacking possibilities.

15	...	b4
16	♘d5	e6
17	♘xf6+	♕xf6

The advantage of the two bishops, the half-open c-file, and the active placement of his pieces guarantee Black an excellent game.

18	hg	hg
19	♕h2	♖fc8

Black not only avoids mate but also creates the threat of 20 ... ♖xc2+ 21 ♘xc2 ♕xb2+.

20	♕xd6?!	*(164)*

Evidently White was expecting 20 ... ♖xc2+, when he would have replied 21 ♔b1. But Black now played a move which White had not foreseen.

20	...	e5!

It turns out that 21 ♕xf6 ♗xf6 22 ♘b3 ♖xc2+ 23 ♔b1 ♗b5 leads to an advantage for Black, but all the same this was the line that White should have chosen.

21	♕xd7?	ed
22	♗xd4	

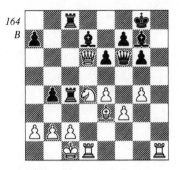

It was no use playing 22 ♖xd4, in view of 22 ... ♕xf3.

22	...	♕g5+
23	♔b1	♗xd4

Now on 24 ♖xd4 Black wins with 24 ... ♖xc2 25 ♖dd1 ♕e5.

| 24 | b3 *(165)* |

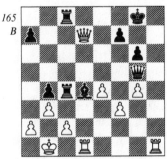

| 24 | ... | ♖d8! |

This is the point!

25	♕b7	♖c3
26	♕xb4	♗g7
27	♖xd8+	♕xd8

Material is theoretically equal, but White's position is hopeless.

| 28 | f4 | ♖h3! |

The black rook cannot be captured, because of mate on the back rank. In the event of 29 ♖c1 (29 ♖f1 is bad because of 29 ... ♖f3, and so is 29 ♖g1 in view of 29 ... ♖g3) decisive is 29 ... ♗c3 30 ♕c5 ♕d2 (with the threat 30 ... ♕xc1+) 31 ♖f1 ♕xf4!.

White resigned.

Game No. 56
Maric–Gligoric
Belgrade 1962

1	e4	c5
2	♘f3	d6
3	d4	cd
4	♘xd4	♘f6
5	♘c3	a6
6	♗g5	e6
7	f4	♕b6
8	♕d2	♕xb2
9	♖b1	♕a3

One of the most popular variations of the Sicilian Defence which has caused quite a few disputes among theoreticians and was a menacing weapon in Fischer's hands.

10 ♗xf6

A positional attempt to refute the Fischer Variation. It is generally considered that the most promising continuation for White is 10 f5.

10	...	gf
11	♗e2	♘c6
12	♘xc6	

A fashionable continuation at that time. White saves a tempo for the sake of rapid development.

12	...	bc
13	0–0	♕a5!

Giving check on the square c5 gives White, in Gligoric's opinion, an opportunity for the manoeuvre ♘c3–a4–b6, and in any case the white king will have to move off the open diagonal. The move in the game pins the knight on c3, takes control of the fifth rank and brings the queen nearer to the danger-zone around Black's own king.

14	♔h1	♗e7
15	f5	ef
16	ef	♗xf5?! *(166)*

During the game Gligoric supposed that the line he had found would lead to a solution of Black's opening problems. But, as was later discovered, after 17 ♗xa6! White has the advantage.

| 17 | ♗f3?! | 0–0! |

A crafty trap, into which White falls.

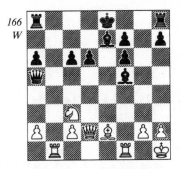

18	**♗xc6**	**♖ac8**	

Foreseeing a decisive combination.

19	**♗b7**	**♖xc3**
20	**♖xf5** *(167)*	

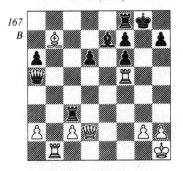

Now after 20 ... ♕xf5 21 ♕xc3 White has an excellent position, but ... lightning strikes from out of the blue.

          20   ...   **♖b3!!**

Black's rook has moved to a square where it is attacked three times (and without even capturing anything!), and in addition Black's queen is twice *en prise*, but the weakness of the back rank is what really decides matters.

White resigned.

12   The Intermediate Move

The term 'intermediate move' (or *Zwischenzug*) is usually applied to an unexpected move which, at first sight, does not follow logically from the position but which is capable of abruptly disturbing the planned course of events or of cutting short a forced variation. Players most often fail to notice an intermediate move during an exchange, when the recapture of a piece (or pawn) seems to be a matter of course.

For example, in the game Nagy–Balogh, Hungary 1948, after the moves 1 e4 c5 2 b4 cb 3 d4 e5 4 de ♘c6 5 ♘f3 ♘ge7 6 ♗f4 (better was 6 ♗b2) 6 ... ♘g6 7 ♗g3 ♕a5 8 ♕d5 *(168)* a position arose in which White, so it would appear, has suppressed the active operations of the black pieces, primarily of the queen.

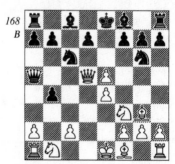

At first sight, Black's next move, **8 ... b3+!**, gives the impression of being a mistake. But after the natural 9 ♕xa5 (9 ♘bd2 is bad, because of 9 ... ♕c3!) there followed the stunning intermediate move 9 ... b2!!, and after 10 ♕c3 ♗b4 11 ♕xb4 ♘xb4 White resigned.

Game No. 57
Spassky–Capelan
Solingen 1974

1	e4	c5
2	♘f3	e6
3	d4	cd
4	♘xd4	a6
5	♗d3	♗c5
6	♘b3	♗a7
7	♘c3	♘c6
8	♕e2	d6
9	♗e3	♗xe3
10	♕xe3	♘f6
11	0–0–0	0–0
12	f4	

A different plan was tried in the game Tseshkovsky–Suetin, Sochi 1980: 12 ♗e2 ♕c7 13 g4 b5 14 g5 ♘e8 15 f4 ♖b8 16 ♖d2 b4 17 ♘a4 ♘e7 18 ♖hd1 ♕c6 (18 ... ♗d7 19 e5!) 19 ♕a7 ♖b7 20 ♕xa6 ♕xe4 with a good game for Black.

12	...	♕c7

The queen gets off the d-file, since White threatened 13 e5. In the event of 12 ... e5 13 f5 b5 14 ♗e2 b4 15 ♘a4 ♕c7 16 g4 ♗d7 17 g5 White has the advantage (Christoph–Hollis, Hastings 1965/66).

13	♖hg1

In the game T. Georgadze–Böhlig, Halle 1978, White preferred a questionable pawn sacrifice: 13 g4. In the event of acceptance of the sacrifice with 13 ... ♘xg4, Georgadze quotes the variation 14 ♕g3 ♘f6 15 ♖dg1 ♘e8 16 h4, reckoning that White has sufficient compensation for the pawn.

However, it is not easy for White to create real threats. On 16 e5 de 17 ♘e4, possible is 17 ... f5, and 16 f5 ♕e7 is good for Black. In all cases a complicated struggle lies ahead, with chances for both sides.

13	...	♖d8

The most energetic continuation is considered to be 13 ... e5. Black should create counterplay on the queenside as quickly as he can.

14	g4	d5
15	e5	d4

16	♕f2

In the event of 16 ♕h3 dc 17 ef the black queen would take the pawn on f4 with check.

| 16 | ... | dc |
| 17 | ef | ♘b4 *(169)* |

Threatening to exchange the bishop and thereby eliminate the threat of 18 ♕h4. But White stunned his opponent with a thunderbolt.

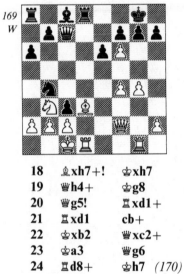

169
W

18	♗xh7+!	♔xh7
19	♕h4+	♔g8
20	♕g5!	♖xd1+
21	♖xd1	cb+
22	♔xb2	♕xc2+
23	♔a3	♕g6
24	♖d8+	♔h7 *(170)*

The impression is that Black has warded off the attack, but the main surprise for him is still to come.

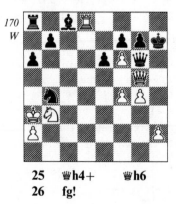

170
W

| 25 | ♕h4+ | ♕h6 |
| 26 | fg! | |

It was on this intermediate move that the whole of White's far-sighted combination was based!

26	...	♚xg7
27	♖g8+	♚xg8
28	♕xh6	♘c6
29	♘c5	♘e7
30	♘e4	♘d5
31	g5	Black resigned.

There is no defence against 32 ♘f6+ followed by checkmate.

13 Combining Tactical Methods

Very often tactical operations are based on more than one idea. For example, exploiting the weakness of the back rank is in many cases associated with the deflection of the pieces defending it. Other ways of combining tactical methods are also possible.

In the well-known game Fischer–Reshevsky, USA Ch. 1958/59, after 1 e4 c5 2 ♘f3 ♘c6 3 d4 cd 4 ♘xd4 g6 5 ♗e3 ♗g7 6 ♘c3 ♘f6 7 ♗c4 0–0 8 ♗b3 Black decided to exchange off the white bishop and played 8 ... ♘a5?, after which there followed 9 e5 ♘e8 *(171)*.

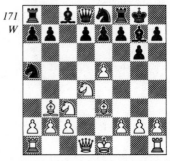

And here lightning struck from out of the blue: **10 ♗xf7+!** ♚xf7 (if 10 ... ♖xf7 then 11 ♘e6, winning the queen) 11 ♘e6!. A combination involving enticement of the black king and a pin along the d-file. Now in the event of 11 ... ♚xe6 there follows 12 ♕d5+ ♚f5 13 g4+ ♚xg4 14 ♖g1+ ♚h5 15 ♕d1+ with mate. White soon won.

Enticement plus Deflection

Game No. 58
Sveshnikov–A. Sokolov
Sochi 1983

	1	e4	c5
	2	c3	

A move which characterises the variation bearing the name of the famous Russian master, Alapin, and which in recent years has become fashionable, largely as a result of Sveshnikov's efforts.

	2	...	d5
	3	ed	♕xd5
	4	d4	e6
	5	♘f3	♘f6
	6	♘a3	♗e7

The simple 6 ... ♕d8 would guarantee Black comfortable equality.

	7	♘b5	♘a6
	8	c4	♕e4+?!

Black complies with his opponent's plans.

	9	♗e2	cd
	10	0–0	0–0
	11	♗d3	♕g4
	12	♖e1!	

It turns out that the black queen is in a very unfortunate position: the threat is 13 h3 ♕h5 14 ♖e5.

	12	...	♘d7
	13	♗e2	♕g6
	14	♘fxd4	♖d8

Not a very prudent move. More accurate was 14 ... ♕f6 followed by 15 ... e5.

	15	♗h5	♕f6 *(172)*

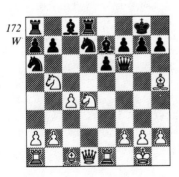

In this apparently quiet position White's next move was like a crash of thunder on a clear day.

16   ♗g5!!   ♕xg5
17   ♗xf7+!

With his previous move White sacrificed a bishop in order to deflect the black queen away from the f7-square and entice it onto g5. And now the other bishop offers itself up, in order to destroy Black's fortifications and bring the black king out into the centre.

17   ...   ♔xf7
18   ♘xe6   ♕g6!

A natural continuation, which gives Black some hope for resistance. By playing 18 ... ♕f6 Black would have taken away an important square from his own king.

19   ♕d5 *(173)*

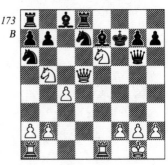

The first impression is that this move ends the game. After 19 ... ♔e8 decisive is 20 ♘d6+ ♗xd6 21 ♕xd6 ♔f7 22 ♘xd8+ ♔g8 23 ♕d5+. All the same, Black still has defensive resources.

19   ...   ♘f6!
20   ♘xd8++   ♔f8

Of course, not 20 ... ♔e8 because of 21 ♖xe7+.

21   ♕e5   ♗c5!

The start of counter-attacking operations.

22   ♘d4   ♔g8
23   ♘8e6?!

White overlooks the strongest move — 23 ♖e3!, when after 23 ... ♗d7 he has the simple 24 ♘xb7. There could have followed: 24 ... ♖e8 25 ♕f4 ♖xe3 26 fe ♗xd4 27 ed ♗c6 28 d5 ♗xb7 29 ♕d4 with a difficult game for Black.

23   ...   ♗xe6

24	♕xe6+	♔h8
25	♘b3	h6

Black opens an escape-hole just in case, but it is possible that 25 ... ♗b6 was stronger.

	26	♖e5? *(174)*

But this is a tactical error. The simple 26 ♘xc5 ♘xc5 27 ♕d6 would have maintained White's advantage.

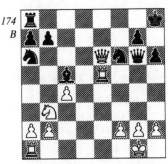

26	...	♗xf2+!
27	♔xf2	♖e8
28	♕f5	♘g4+
29	♕xg4	

Alas, White has to part with his queen, after which it is hard for him to reckon on victory.

29	...	♕xg4
30	♖xe8+	♔h7
31	♔g1	♘b4
32	♖ae1	♘d3?!

Black wrongly rejects the natural 32 ... ♕xc4.

33	♖8e4!	♕g6
34	♖1e2	♘xb2
35	h3	♘d1
36	♖d4!	

Now that the white pieces have become better coordinated Black's position quickly deteriorates.

36	...	♘c3
37	♖e7	♕f5
38	♖g4	

Avoiding a simple trap: 38 ♖dd7 ♘e2+!.

38	...	♕f6

39	♖xb7	♘e2+
40	♔h2	♕e5+
41	g3	

It turns out that Black cannot play 41 ... ♕e3, because of mate in three (42 ♖bxg7+ ♔h8 43 ♖g8+ ♔h7 44 ♖4g7 mate).

41	...	h5
42	♖bxg7+	

On 42 ... ♔h8, there follows 43 ♖7g5 ♕e8 44 ♖xh5+ ♕xh5 45 ♖h4.

Black resigned.

Enticement plus Deflection plus Interference

Game No. 59
Nunn–Murshed
London 1985

1	e4	c5
2	♘f3	♘c6
3	d4	cd
4	♘xd4	e6
5	♘c3	d6
6	♗e3	♘f6
7	♗c4	♗e7
8	♕e2	a6
9	0–0–0	

This system requires extremely accurate and forceful play from both sides.

9	...	♕c7
10	♗b3	♘a5

A very common continuation is 10 ... 0–0 (see Games 11, 12, 37, 42 and 49). Here too, play is extremely sharp.

11	g4	b5
12	g5	♘xb3+

It is a mistake to play 12 ... ♘d7, in view of 13 ♗xe6!.

13	ab	♘d7
14	h4	

The sacrifice of a piece with 14 ♘f5 is extremely tempting, but practice has shown that it is not sufficient to obtain an advantage. After 14 ... ef 15 ♘d5 ♕d8 16 ef ♗b7 17 f6 gf 18 ♖he1 ♗xd5 19 ♖xd5 ♖g8! the most White can reckon on is 20 ♗f4 ♔f8 21

♕h5 ♕a5 22 ♕e2 ♕d8 23 ♕h5 and a draw by repetition.

14	...	b4
15	♘a4	♘c5
16	h5	e5

A crucial decision. More well-founded from a positional point of view was the continuation 16 ... ♗d7 17 g6 ♗f6 18 gf+ ♔xf7, when Black has sufficient counterplay.

17	♘f5	♗xf5

Black loses after 17 ... ♘xe4, because of 18 ♗b6, and also bad for Black is 17 ... ♘xb3+ 18 ♔b1 ♘c5 19 ♘xc5 dc 20 g6. But worth considering was 17 ... 0–0.

18	ef	♘xa4

White gets a considerable advantage after 18 ... ♘xb3+ 19 ♔b1 ♘c5 20 ♕c4.

19	ba	♕c6?!

A significant inaccuracy. It looks better to play the natural 19 ... b3 20 ♔b1 bc+ 21 ♕xc2 ♕xc2 22 ♔xc2 ♗d7 23 b3 ♖hc8+ 24 ♔b2 ♖ab8, when White's advantage is not too great. But apparently stronger still is 19 ... ♖c8 followed by 20 ... ♕c4.

20	♔b1!	♕xa4
21	♖h4	

The immediate 21 f6 would give White nothing, because of 21 ... b3! 22 cb ♕e4+.

21	...	♖b8

Attempting to halt White's pawn offensive on the kingside would not have led to anything good for Black, as after 21 ... h6 there could have followed 22 f6! hg 23 fg ♖g8 24 h6!, and if 21 ... f6 then 22 h6!.

22	♖d5	♕d7
23	♕d3	

White intends after 24 b3 and 25 ♖c4 to get complete control of the centre.

23	...	b3
24	cb	0–0
25	f6?!	

There was no need to hurry. White could have quietly moved his rook on h4 to h1 and then played g5–g6 at his leisure. On 25 ♖xe5 there could have followed 25 ... f6!.

25	...	gf
26	gf	♗xf6

27	♖xd6	♛e7
28	♖g4+	♚h8
29	♗c5	♖fd8
30	♛d5 *(175)*	

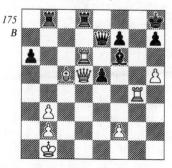

Black has defended a difficult position well, and now with 30 ... ♖b5! could have forced White to transpose to an equal ending. In the event of 31 ♛c6? White would even have lost, as his rook on g4 is undefended: 31 ... ♖xc5! 32 ♖xd8+ ♛xd8 33 ♛xc5 ♛d1+.

30	...	♖xd6?
31	♗xd6	♛d7 *(176)*

The impression is that Black's plan has been successful, since the rook on g4 is now attacked and the bishop on d6 is pinned. White cannot play 32 ♗xe5 because of 32 ... ♛f5+ (this is why Black put his queen on d7 and not on d8).

32 ♛xe5!

This rather straightforward tactical trick radically changes the nature of the game. Of course, White's queen cannot be taken.

32	...	♛d8

33	♕g3	♖b5
34	h6	♖d5
35	♗c7	♕e8
36	♔a2!	

The king is moved to a safe place, and now White threatens the decisive manoeuvre ♖g4–b4–b8.

36	...	♖d2 *(177)*

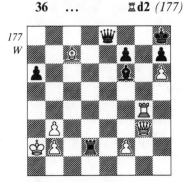

| 37 | ♗e5!! | |

A move of exceptional beauty and power, combining several tactical methods and motifs (enticement, deflection, interference, exploiting the cramped position of the black king). On 37 ... ♗xe5 there follows 38 ♖g8+! (the queen is deflected from the defence of the bishop) 38 ... ♕xg8 39 ♕xe5+.

37	...	♖xf2
38	♖e4	

Simpler was 38 ♗xf6+ ♖xf6 39 ♕c3 ♕d8 40 ♖f4.

38	...	♗xe5 *(178)*

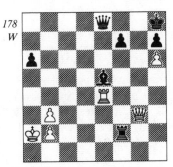

And now a really elegant conclusion.

| 38 | ♕g7+!! | Black resigned. |

Index of Variations

(Numbers refer to *page* numbers)

3) Scheveningen Variation
1 e4 c5 2 ♘f3 d6 3 d4 cxd4 4 ♘xd4 ♘f6 5 ♘c3 e6

6 f4 ♗e7 7 ♕f3 *89*
6 ... a6 7 ♗d3 *177*
6 ♗e3 ♘c6 7 f4 ♗e7 8 ♕f3 *155*
6 ... a6 7 ♕d2 b5 *76*
　　　　7 f3 ♘c6 8 g4 ♗e7 9 ♕d2 0–0 10 0–0–0 ♘xd4 *56*
　　　　　　　　　　10 ... ♖b8 *187*
6 g4 ♘c6 7 g5 ♘d7 8 ♗e3 ♗e7 9 h4 0–0 *143*
6 ... a6 7 g5 ♘fd7 8 h4 *158*
6 ♗e2 a6 7 ♗e3 ♕c7 8 a4 *73*
　　　　7 0–0 ♕c7 8 ♗e3 ♗e7 9 f4 ♘c6 10 ♕e1 ♗d7 *24*
　　　　　　　　　　10 ... 0–0 *27*

4) Richter–Rauzer Attack
1 e4 c5 2 ♘f3 d6 3 d4 cxd4 4 ♘xd4 ♘f6 5 ♘c3 ♘c6 6 ♗g5

6 ... e6 7 ♕d2 a6 8 0–0–0 h6 *67*
　　　　7 ... ♗e7 8 0–0–0 0–0 9 ♘b3 ♕b6 *102*
　　　　　　　　　9 ... a6 *185*

5) Sozin Attack
1 e4 c5 2 ♘f3 d6 3 d4 cxd4 4 ♘xd4 ♘f6 5 ♘c3 ♘c6 6 ♗c4

6 ... ♕b6 *105*
6 ... e6 7 ♗e3 a6 8 ♗b3 ♘a5 *112*
　　　　7 ... ♗e7 8 ♗b3 0–0 9 ♕e2 ♕a5 *109*
　　　　　　　8 ♕e2 a6 9 0–0–0 ♕c7 10 ♗b3 ♘a5 *204*
　　　　　　　　　　10 ... 0–0
11 ♖hg1 ♘a5 *47*
11 ... ♘d7 12 ♕h5 *150*
　　　　　12 g4 *173*
11 g4 ♘xd4 12 ♖xd4 b5 13 g5 ♘d7 14 ♖g1 *49*
　　　　　　　　14 f4 *132*